Issues
in Cultural
Diversity

Harold Troper and Lee Palmer

Canadian Critical Issues Series
The Ontario Institute for Studies in Education

THE ONTARIO INSTITUTE FOR STUDIES IN EDUCATION
has three prime functions: to conduct programs of
graduate study in education, to undertake research in
education, and to assist in the implementation of the
findings of educational studies. The Institute is a college
chartered by an Act of the Ontario Legislature in
1965. It is affiliated with the University of Toronto for
graduate studies purposes.
   The publications program of The Ontario Institute
for Studies in Education has been established to make
available information and materials arising from
studies in education, to foster the spirit of critical
inquiry, and to provide a forum for the exchange of
ideas about education. The opinions expressed should be
viewed as those of the contributors.

© The Ontario Institute for Studies in Education 1976
252 Bloor Street West, Toronto, Ontario   M5S 1V6

ISBN 0-7744-0124-9   Printed in Canada
1 2 3 4 5 6 BP 18 08 97 87 77 67

Contents

Editors' Preface

The Canadian Critical Issues Series has grown out of the Canadian Public Issues Project, which was initiated at the Ontario Institute for Studies in Education early in the summer of 1969. The purpose of the project was to stimulate discussion and reflection about controversial issues in contemporary Canadian society by developing a program focusing on these issues through case studies. Since 1969 the staff of the project have collected materials and written cases about contemporary incidents covering a wide range of problem areas. The cases are, for the most part, based on published reports—newspapers, journals, books, legal documents, and government reports. Many of the topical units have been taught experimentally in high schools in Metropolitan Toronto, Belleville, Ottawa, Timmins, and elsewhere in Canada.

The books, adapted from these units, are intended to be both provocative and informative. Case studies are followed by questions and analogy situations designed to stimulate reflection and discussion about the broader issues they raise. Additional factual information is included to bring other perspectives to bear on the cases and the problems they represent. Each book concludes with a selected bibliography of reference and resource materials in print and on film and tape.

John Eisenberg
Harold Troper
Editors

Authors' Preface

It is both a cliché and a truism to say that Canada is a nation of minorities, a nation in which many racial, religious, ethnic, and linguistic groups coexist and make their home. This variety of traditions and life-styles is increasingly acknowledged to add immeasurably to the rich fabric of Canadian life. Yet, on occasion, this very richness generates issues or dilemmas for minority groups, individual group members, and Canadian society in general—issues and dilemmas which test the national resolve to social justice, equality of opportunity, tolerance, and respect for differences.

Issues in Cultural Diversity details a series of cases in which the concerns of minority groups, individuals, or the wider Canadian community are brought into critical focus. We begin by examining the Hutterites, a group which maintains a relatively isolated rural existence. Next we explore the end of an isolated black neighborhood in Halifax and then move on to outline one black man's efforts to rent an apartment in Toronto. We also center our attention on the economic, social, and political consequences of minority issues surrounding events that took place outside the Ontario Science Centre in Toronto, in Fort St. James, British Columbia, and in St. Leonard, a suburb of Montreal. Lastly we look at immigration itself, and the role it continues to play in shaping the Canadian population.

These cases, and the questioning framework which follows each case, do not pretend to cover all aspects of minority life in Canada. It is hoped, however, that they will act as a catalyst to discussion, not just of the specific items raised but of the wider implications which grow out of the specific cases under consideration.

This book would not have been possible without the funds allocated by OISE to the project. We especially wish to acknowledge the support and assistance given by John Main, head of the Publication Division, and Trevor Wigney, past chairman of the Department of History and Philosophy of Education. We also wish to thank the many graduate students at OISE and high-school teachers who assisted in the research, teaching, and evaluation of case materials for the project. We are grateful to John Eisenberg and Eydie Troper for their contributions to this volume, to Peggy Bristow for her assistance in typing the manuscript, and to Rene Salsberg for her rare combination of patience and good humor in editing the authors' work.

H. T.
L. P.

1

The Hutterites and
Their Neighbors

Because February is normally a bitter cold month in Alberta, it is not the usual season for civic holidays or outdoor meetings. But 1973 proved an exception for the town of Vulcan and its surrounding area when Friday, 23 February was declared a civic holiday by the Vulcan town council. Schools and many business establishments in the area remained closed.

Residents of Vulcan did have a very special reason to celebrate, since 1973 marked the sixtieth anniversary of the incorporation of Vulcan as a town, the local administrative seat for the first county organized in Alberta. Celebration, however, was not the reason for this civic holiday. Its purpose was to allow the local population to attend a protest demonstration in Edmonton, the provincial capital, more than 250 miles to the north.

Vulcan is not a big town by national standards. Situated seventy miles southeast of Calgary on the Canadian Pacific Railway line to Lethbridge, it has a population of about 2,000. Sitting as it does in the heart of a rich grain-growing region, Vulcan is the major business and social center for the neighboring farm population of

1

about 8,000 persons, who look upon the town as their own.

It is probably safe to say that without the farmers who live in the vicinity of Vulcan the town could not exist; in fact, it would not have a reason to exist. Farmers from the surrounding area need the town to do business, shop, and meet with neighbors. Town merchants in turn depend on the surrounding farm community for their livelihood. This mutual dependence had been natural for so long that probably few people in Vulcan gave it much thought—at least not until 1973.

Early that year, residents of Vulcan and other similar small towns began to fear that their prosperity, if not their very survival, was threatened. The cause for this concern was the Alberta government's plan to revoke existing legislation restricting Hutterite land purchases.

The Hutterite Brethren are a small agricultural Christian sect who trace their origins back to the sixteenth-century German Reformation. From their earliest beginnings the Hutterites practiced both pacifism (refusing to take up weapons for any cause) and agricultural collectivism (settling on communal farms where all property is owned in common). Believing that this is the way that Christ wanted his followers to live, they point to the New Testament, Acts 2 : 44, as the foundation for their religious and communal behavior: "All the believers had all things in communal possession; they sold whatever they had and divided the proceeds to all, according as they had need." Through a literal interpretation of this passage the Hutterites gradually developed their particular form of Christian collective farm life.

Because of their pacifist beliefs and communal lifestyle, the Hutterites were frequently persecuted by their neighbors and forced to move from one place to another in search of peace. Retaining their distinct German dialect as the language of education, communication, and prayer, the Hutterites fled eastward across Europe.

Over a period of 200 years they passed through Moravia, Slovakia, and Transylvania into Russia.

The move into Russia seemed to promise safe, secure, peaceful homes for Hutterites. In 1770 Catherine the Great invited several agricultural groups, including the Hutterites, to colonize the empty lands of the Ukraine, north of the Black Sea. The Hutterites established collective farms (which they refer to as colonies), practiced their religion, operated their own schools, and preserved their German language and religious culture. Then, in 1864, for reasons of state which did not originally involve the Hutterites, the Russian government passed legislation making Russian the only language of instruction in schools and placing all schools under state supervision. The government further announced that universal and compulsory military service would be instituted. The Hutterites could accept none of these regulations and once again they were on the move.

In 1874 the Hutterite Brethren began a migration to the United States. They gradually established colonies in South Dakota and Montana. Again, these Hutterite communities ran into difficulty, this time in the heat of World War I. When the U.S. joined World War I, about 1,700 Hutterites in the United States lived on seventeen farm colonies, relatively isolated from their neighbors. However, the refusal of Hutterites to serve in the American military, their continued everyday use of the German language, and their "foreign" ways quickly generated hostility among their once friendly neighbors.

Fearing persecution, Hutterite leadership once again began to look elsewhere for new homes. Beginning in 1918, most of the Hutterites in the United States moved north to seek refuge in Canada. The majority settled in Alberta. By 1922 they had established fourteen colonies in Alberta and today the number of colonies in that province has grown to about seventy-five.

Hutterite life in Canada centers around the colony.

Each colony attempts to be self-reliant, meeting as many of its members' needs as possible. While the Hutterites farm with the most modern machinery available, individual material goods like clothing and furniture are kept to a minimum—there are, for example, few if any radios and televisions and very little variety in clothing styles. Much of what Hutterites do possess, they make for themselves.

Most Hutterite children are educated in schools on their own colony by a Hutterite teacher trained in a near-by teachers' college, or by an outsider brought in to teach in the colony's school.

No Hutterite owns land of his own. Land is owned collectively by a colony, which buys goods it cannot produce, sells produce for its members, and, in this way, supplies all the members' needs. For instance, colonies (such as those near Vulcan) have no private kitchens; instead, there is a central dining hall serving all members.

Because each colony takes care of its own needs, Hutterites do not usually seek nor accept much in the way of government assistance. It is interesting to note that Hutterites do not, as a rule, take baby bonus payments, old age pensions, or similar benefits even though they pay income taxes and are legally entitled to benefits.

By Hutterite tradition, it is not considered acceptable for colonies to grow beyond a maximum population of 150 persons. Shortly after the population reaches 100, the colony splits if possible. New land is purchased and members draw lots to decide which families will move to the new colony and which will stay behind. Livestock and other goods are divided and soon a "daughter colony" is established on its own.

A colony cannot split, however, if it is unable to purchase lands on which to establish the daughter colony. It is the problem of finding land for new colonies and acquiring additional land for existing colonies which has continually caused friction between the Hutterites and

4

their neighbors, including those in the Vulcan area.

As happened during their stay in the United States, friction between Hutterites and non-Hutterites became aggravated by a war situation. During World War II the Hutterites again appeared suspect. Young Hutterites refused to serve in the military (although many accepted alternate service in such areas as federal forestry projects), they refused to contribute to wartime money-raising campaigns or buy victory bonds, and they were conspicuous in their continued use of the language of the enemy, German.

In 1942 the Social Credit government of Alberta responded to anti-Hutterite feeling by passing legislation to forbid the sale of land to the Hutterites. The following year leasing of land to Hutterites was also disallowed. After the war, in 1947, the Alberta government passed a modified Communal Property Act. This Act prevented any existing colony from expanding beyond its 1944 area. In effect, no new colonies could be established with more than 6,400 acres and nobody could sell land to Hutterites unless the land had already been on sale for ninety days, during which time the government would offer financial assistance to non-Hutterite purchasers.

In 1959 a Communal Property Control Board was set up to evaluate all land purchase applications from Hutterites. Final permission to buy land was only granted in a case where the application could meet special standards judged on the basis of whether or not the purchase was "in the public interest." Generally, this meant that proposed colonies were to be a minimum of fifteen miles apart. No more than two colonies would be permitted in the same municipality and no more than 5 percent of land in a municipality should be in Hutterite hands. While this severely handicapped and slowed Hutterite expansion it did not stop it completely.

The election of a Conservative government in Alberta in 1971 brought about a dramatic change. During the

5

election the Conservatives promised that if elected they would enact a provincial Bill of Rights. It was quite evident to both Hutterites and non-Hutterites alike that any such provincial Bill of Rights would likely be in conflict with the restrictions on Hutterite expansion—the restrictions obviously and directly discriminated against one religious group. A Bill of Rights which guaranteed freedom of religion would make it difficult if not impossible to continue with anti-Hutterite legislation.

To the people in and around Vulcan the threat posed by the new government's proposed Bill of Rights seemed grave indeed. While merchants in Vulcan claimed they could live with the existing Hutterite colonies in the area, they feared that more new colonies would prove disastrous to their town as it had already been to the town of Brant, Alberta. They alleged that customers lost by Brant merchants, as farmers who sold land moved out and Hutterites who did not buy from local merchants moved in, eventually put many Brant merchants out of business.

It was pointed out that Hutterites already competed with local merchants. Dave Uhl, assistant manager of the local I.G.A. grocery store, claimed that Hutterites near Vulcan not only did not purchase food from his store but brought their own farm goods into town and sold them to the public door-to-door in direct competition with his I.G.A. store, often at cheaper prices.

With the coming end to restrictions on Hutterite property purchases, Vulcan merchants and local farmers waited with apprehension for new Hutterite colonies to spring up in the area. They feared for their town if local merchants could not survive, and for their schools if student population declined as local farmers sold out and Hutterites kept their children in their own schools.

In a final attempt to stop the repeal of existing anti-Hutterite legislation, the Vulcan town council, in co-operation with other local towns, declared the civic holiday on 23 February 1973. Citizens of the area were

6

encouraged to travel to Edmonton for a protest. Before sunrise on that frosty day three chartered buses, followed by fifteen private cars, started up Highway 24 carrying demonstrators to the provincial capital five hours' drive and more than 250 miles to the north.

In Edmonton, the anti-Hutterite protestors assembled on the steps in front of the legislative building in the early afternoon. One leader of the protest, Dave Mitchell, a drugstore owner in Vulcan, went inside and presented a brief to Premier Peter Lougheed and several members of his newly elected cabinet. Meanwhile protestors waited outside in the freezing temperature.

The premier promised nothing. The anti-Hutterite legislation was a dead issue as far as he was concerned; it would officially expire one week after the demonstration. The new provincial Bill of Rights, he explained, must take precedence.

Still concerned for the future of their town, the protestors from Vulcan turned around and went away empty-handed. It was dark when they arrived home after the long drive. A week later restrictions on Hutterite land purchases ceased to exist.

The Issues

• Should Hutterite land purchases be restricted?

Vulcan, Alberta
• Do you believe that increased Hutterite land expansion represents any real threat to the town of Vulcan? Why or why not?

• Imagine yourself to be each of the following Vulcan town residents. How do you think you would feel about new Hutterite colonies in the neighborhood?
   –a farmer who wants to sell his land and retire
   –a farmer who wishes to buy land to expand his farm

7

- the owner of a small clothing store
- a local doctor
- the operator of a gasoline station
- a student in the local high school
- the member of the Alberta legislature for the provincial riding of which Vulcan is a part

• Can you think of other persons usually found in a small town like Vulcan who would be opposed to new Hutterite colonies in their area?

• Can you think of any persons in the town who would benefit from the creation of new colonies?

• Do you think that any local residents would be completely unaffected by the establishment of new colonies? State your reasons for each choice.

• Do you believe that the Vulcan town council acted properly in supporting and helping to organize the protest demonstration in Edmonton? Why or why not?

• What else could they do to make their dissatisfaction known to the provincial government?

• Once a democratically elected provincial government makes a decision is it right for citizens to protest against it? Why or why not?

• Must citizens of towns like Vulcan just accept distant government decisions which they feel will directly affect their lives in a negative way?

• For many years provincial government legislation negatively affected the lives of Hutterites. Is the new situation simply a reversal of injustice between the town and the Hutterites?

• Do you believe that the end to restrictions on Hutterite land purchases will be more harmful or less harmful to the town's survival than the continued restrictions would be to Hutterite survival? Explain your answer.

• If you were forced to choose, which would take

precedence—the continued prosperity of Vulcan or the right of Hutterites to expand their colonies? Explain your choice.

Related Factors

• The Vulcan town council and local merchants feared that new Hutterite colonies around Vulcan would undermine the town's prosperity and drive population out. Some people have pointed to other factors which might be affecting prosperity or stability of towns like Vulcan. What do you think could be the impact on Vulcan of the following?

–In recent years better highways and more leisure time have allowed local farm families to drive a greater distance to do their weekly shopping. In the case of Vulcan it is a simple matter for farmers who once shopped in Vulcan to drive to big shopping centers and department stores in Calgary only 70 miles away.

–After finishing high school in smaller towns across Canada, many young people are moving to cities to attend university or for greater employment oppor-make it easy for them to return to their small towns tunities. While some enter professions which would or to farms, many do not. As a result, many young men and women from an area such as the Vulcan district choose to stay in bigger cities. Consequently, population in rural areas has shown a slow but steady decline relative to urban areas.

–Related to the loss of youth to towns like Vulcan is the loss of retired citizens. While in earlier years a farmer who retired might have stayed on his farm with a son or daughter who took over the farm, or moved into the local town, today many farmers are retiring to cities where their children have resettled. Others are using their savings and pensions to move to warmer climates like British Columbia or the southern United States for their retirement years.

This also helps to lower population in small towns like Vulcan.

—Farm lands sold in Canada today do not always go into the hands of another farm family. Big business has moved into agriculture operating what are often called corporate farms. A company might, for instance, buy a series of farms over a large area and employ a team of mobile workmen with modern equipment to go from farm to farm taking care of the crops. Ranches and poultry farms may be operated like large automated factories employing few people. The company, of course, buys its necessities and sells its produce in bulk, usually by-passing any local town like Vulcan.

• Can you think of any other factors which might be creating economic difficulties for merchants or citizens of small towns like Vulcan which have not been noted?

• How important do you think the Hutterite situation is, compared to these other factors affecting small towns like Vulcan?

The Hutterites

• Do you believe that the Hutterites should be completely free to decide on their style of life and degree of involvement in the community?

• Should Hutterites adjust in any way to local conditions?

• What do you think the Hutterites could or should do to make themselves more welcome in the Vulcan area?

• Which of the following do you think it would be possible for the Hutterites to do and still remain faithful to their way of life? Which would not be possible? Explain your decision in each case.

—buy all their goods in Vulcan
—not sell their products in competition with Vulcan merchants

10

    –stop making their own clothing and furniture
    –send their children to schools off the Hutterite colony
    –speak only English
    –dress like everyone else
    –give up communal living and move to family farms
    –join the military if Canada goes to war

• Can any group such as the Hutterites really expect to live in Canada and remain largely unaffected by the Canadian way of life? Explain your answer.

• Do you believe that groups like the Hutterites should be allowed (or encouraged) to continue their traditional way of life once they come to Canada?

• Does Canada have a right to demand that groups like the Hutterites give up their traditional way of life? Why or why not?

• What could the government do to encourage or discourage groups like the Hutterites in their efforts to keep their own way of life?

• Does government have any role in this area at all? Do the schools have any role? If so, what is it?

• Hutterites live in colonies in rural Canada. What do you think the situation would be if Hutterites decided to build and operate factories as collectives in cities as they do farms in rural areas?

• What would the following people feel about such a factory?
    –the owner of a competing factory
    –a worker in a competing factory
    –a homeowner next door to a Hutterite collective home
    –a member of the local board of education
    –a local television salesman
    –the alderman in the district where Hutterites lived

• What do you think would be the response of a similar

group of people in an urban area where the Hutterites decided to set up a "daughter factory"? What action, if any, do you believe they would take to welcome or stop the Hutterite daughter factory?

Freedom of Religion

• The laws restricting Hutterite land purchase were judged to be in violation of the new Alberta Bill of Rights which guaranteed freedom of religion. Do you believe that the Communal Property Act of 1947 restricting Hutterite land purchases was a violation of Hutterite freedom of religion?

• In the following cases what is more important, the right to practice one's religion according to personal belief or the restrictions made on these practices by man-made laws?

Parallel Situation 1

Many observant Seventh Day Adventists and Jews keep Saturday as the Sabbath. They do not work or keep their businesses open; rather, they make Saturday a day of rest and prayer.

For some Seventh Day Adventists and Jews there is a financial hardship in keeping their businesses closed on both Saturday and Sunday. As a result it is not uncommon for those whose business is closed on Saturday to open on Sunday, the Sabbath of the majority of Canadians.

On occasion this produced conflict, especially since many Canadian communities have laws requiring businesses to be closed on Sunday. For their part, Seventh Day Adventists and Jews argue that since Sunday is not their Sabbath they should not be restricted by Sunday closing laws. If they were forced to stay closed on Sundays it could be seen as penalizing them for faithfully keeping their religious traditions.

Opponents of Sunday openings disagree. To allow some people to be open on Sunday while everyone else must be closed gives those few people an unfair business advantage. After all, with everyone else closed on Sunday, the few stores allowed to stay open might do a booming business almost free of competition. In addition, others argue that allowing any businesses to be open on Sunday violates their freedom of religion.

• Should people whose religion requires them to stay closed on Saturday be allowed to open on Sunday?

• Would any of these other proposals solve the problem? Why or why not?
  - keep all businesses closed on Sunday even though businesses owned by Seventh Day Adventists and Jews may also be closed on Saturday
  - allow owners to decide when and how long they will keep their businesses open
  - keep all stores closed on Saturday and Sunday

• Should a majority set up any laws interfering with the religious practices of a minority?

Parallel Situation 2

In recent years one of the most rapidly growing Christian groups has been the Jehovah's Witnesses. Many Canadians and Americans are familiar with the Jehovah's Witnesses' magazines, *Awake* and *The Watchtower*, sold on the street or by door-to-door canvass.

The Jehovah's Witnesses movement has had its share of conflict with the law. One of the areas in which its religious practice has run into clashes with public officials is the area of blood transfusions. Citing the Bible as their authority Jehovah's Witnesses have refused to allow blood transfusions for themselves or their children. Although they accept normal medical treatment in other matters, they interpret Psalms 16 and 1 Chronicles 11: 17–19 as direct prohibitions against taking in the blood

13

of others, either by mouth or medical transfusion.

At times Canadian and American public and medical authorities have been unsure of what action to take when faced by the refusal of a Jehovah's Witness to accept a blood transfusion or allow a transfusion for a child. Increasingly, where the life of a child appears to be in danger as a result of the refusal of the parents to allow a transfusion, parental objections are being ignored. Public and medical officials are using child welfare legislation to remove the child from the authority of the parents in order to give the child the transfusion.

The Jehovah's Witnesses argue that their refusal to accept transfusions for themselves or their children is for religious reasons. To them, if someone dies for lack of a transfusion it might be better than living with a transfusion. Accordingly, they protest that any legal maneuvers used to force transfusions on themselves or their children are a violation of their religious freedom.

In 1972, sixteen-year-old Ricky Green was a patient in the Pennsylvania State Hospital for Crippled Children. Ricky suffered from polio and had a curvature of the spine which prevented him from straightening his body. Doctors recommended an operation to relieve the condition and to prevent Ricky from becoming bedridden for life. Ricky's mother consented to the operation on one condition. Because she was a Jehovah's Witness she demanded that the operation be performed without any blood transfusions. The doctors explained to her that blood transfusions were required, but she held to her condition.

In an effort to carry out the operation the hospital went to court requesting that Ricky be declared a neglected child and that a guardian be appointed who would allow the operation. After a long court battle the Pennsylvania Supreme Court refused the hospital's request. The court ruled that when the child's life is not in immediate danger the parents' religious beliefs must

14

come first. Ricky went without the operation.

• Do you agree with the court's decision in this case? Explain your answer.

• Does forcing transfusions onto Jehovah's Witnesses who do not want them violate their human right to religious freedom? If so, why? If not, why not?

• Should government or medical authorities be allowed to interfere with an individual's religious practices?

• Should they be allowed to interfere in special cases?
  –if a human life is endangered
  –if the refusal of a transfusion comes from a responsible adult who chooses to die for his religious beliefs
  –if the patient is a child whose parents are responsible adults who choose to allow their child to die, if necessary, for religious beliefs
  –if the case is not one of life or death but rather one in which a blood transfusion would enable the patient to recover more quickly and more completely
  –if the patient is going to die anyway, and a blood transfusion will only keep the patient alive a little longer

• Who should make the decision on which is more important, freedom of religion or laws set down by men? Explain your answer.
  –the courts
  –the government
  –the individual who would get the transfusion
  –that individual's wife, husband, or parents
  –religious leaders

2

Africville Removal

In many ways the history of a town or community is similar to the story of a person's life. Like an individual, a town has its date of birth, the date on which it was founded or legally incorporated. A local history, like a biography, will describe a community's early growth, the influences on its development, how and why it prospered, and will detail great events in which the town played a part. As with people, in some cases a change of name may occur—Kitchener, Ontario, for instance, was originally known as Berlin, Ontario. A town entering into amalgamation (union with another town) might also cause a name change—for example, Leaside, Ontario, was amalgamated with the Metropolitan Toronto borough of East York. Unlike people, however, towns rarely cease to exist completely—they rarely die.

Africville died.

In a report prepared for the Institute of Public Affairs, Dalhousie University, Halifax, entitled *Africville Relocation Report*, Donald H. Clairmont and Dennis W. Magill establish the "official" time of death of Africville as 16 January 1964. On that day the Halifax city council accepted the Rose report recommending that Africville be demolished and its residents relocated in Halifax.

Africville was once a town within a town—a small black community in the north corner of the city of Halifax. Africville was officially a part of Halifax although people thought of it as a separate area. At the time Halifax city council approved the relocation project, Africville was home to almost eighty black families, nearly 400 people.

Africville lagged far behind the rest of Halifax in municipal services and general living conditions. Africville was a slum. When the relocation project was approved in 1964, Africville was planted squarely alongside a municipal garbage dump and was bordered on three sides by railway lines and the Bedford Basin port area. On the side of a hill, clusters of small houses in need of repair, outhouses, and small storage shacks were joined by a series of twisting and well-worn footpaths. Africville had no paved roads, no sewer system, no garbage collection, little indoor plumbing, limited heating in winter, and no public school of its own.

City garbage trucks sending up a shower of dust on the dirt road rattled through the community daily on their way to the adjacent garbage dump. At the dump perpetual fires kept clouds of black sooty smoke curling up over the Africville community. Drinking water, such as it was, came from a few private wells that city inspectors had condemned as contaminated. A sign over one well read, "Please Boil This Water Before Drinking and Cooking." Periodically, health inspectors turned the water bloodred with chemicals in an effort to make it safe to drink.

Bringing garbage collection, plumbing, and sewers to Africville could not be done, according to the Halifax Commissioner of Public Works, until Africville homes were moved onto neat rectangular lots. The neighboring garbage dump created an additional problem of rats

18

and the resulting threat of rabies. In the spring of 1965 a complaint about wild dogs sent municipal police into Africville shooting at any dogs they found, including, in this particular incident, a household pet romping beside its owner's home.

The Africville community had not always been a slum. Its history goes back more than 150 years and spans seven or eight generations. Africville was one of several communities founded by black refugees of the War of 1812 who escaped slavery in the United States by coming to Nova Scotia with the assistance of the British military. Africville blacks claimed that their land was a gift from the Crown made in the early 1800s to a freed slave by the name of William Brown. Homes and land holdings were passed down from generation to generation although legal title existed for only a minority of homes.

As it grew, the sprawling city of Halifax finally surrounded the black settlement in Africville. By then, however, the blacks had developed their own unique sense of community, a sense which had matured over generations. Many local residents remembered that their fathers and grandfathers raised goats and chickens in their backyards, flowers and vegetables in the front yard. In the past the old were looked after by the young. When a neighbor was out of work, the Africville community shared food around. Africville residents seldom had to make use of public welfare.

Perhaps because relocation would mean the end of Africville, local residents began to take renewed interest in their history and folklore. According to local tradition the Africville community had survived years of trial and suffering. Stories of victory over oppression were woven into a blend of folksong and folktale passed from generation to generation. In the fifty years before relocation confronted the Africville community, material poverty coexisted with a richness of life. Older residents remembered, for instance, that men in the community would go out at sunrise and come back with enough fish and lobster for all the neighbors. On hot summer nights, before refineries and oil spills fouled the shoreline, people from all over the community would go to the nearby waterfront to swim, then dig for mussels and clams. To outsiders, perhaps, Africville became nothing but a black ghetto, but to the people brought up there it was much more than a place to live. In spite of poor economic conditions, Africville was their home.

Home or not, it became a slum. In spite of the sense of community, the reluctance of the city of Halifax to grant municipal services such as water, sewers, and garbage collection to Africville, poor educational and health facilities, unemployment, and the location of the city dump at the end of the black community all guaranteed slum conditions. By 1963 economic, housing, and sanitary conditions had become so bad that the Halifax Advisory Committee on Human Rights, set up a year earlier to safeguard the rights of Africville citizens, advised the city to commission a study to determine what could be done about Africville. Halifax then engaged Dr. Albert Rose, professor of Social Work at the University of Toronto, to study and recommend solutions to the Africville situation.

Shocked by the terrible conditions it documented, the Rose report proposed that blacks be compensated for their holdings, whether or not they held formal title to the homes, then resettled elsewhere within the city of Halifax and that existing buildings on the site should be demolished. The city accepted the proposal. It was decided that the Africville population be relocated in predominantly white housing developments in the ratio of one black family to five white families. The target date of 31 December 1966 was set for the final elimination of Africville.

At first Africville residents seemed generally in agreement with the plan, but as discussions of compensation began, tension in Africville rose. Local residents who at first argued that they would not be adequately paid for their holdings soon began to grumble that the real reason for razing Africville was to destroy a solid black community in Halifax. Demands that the Africville community be saved gradually grew strident.

Compensation was a problem all of its own. The city claimed it had no legal obligation to compensate those who would be forced to move because no record could be found of the alleged land grant to William Brown. Accordingly, the city argued that most of Africville's residents were "squatters" on city property. However, the city did admit that although it had no legal obligation to compensate residents, it did accept a moral obligation to compensate and assist householders in their forced move. Homes that had been passed among blacks for as little as $500 were being taken over by the city for as much as $4,000. A minimum of $500 became standard. The city even agreed to pay tax arrears and other outstanding bills owed by Africville residents and to give grants to those moving for new furniture and other goods.

As the relocation project grew, blacks became increasingly skeptical. They claimed that the city was trying to steal their land. They argued that once Africville was cleared it could be used for industrial development and the value of their land would soar. They sought compensation on the basis of possible future value of property, not its current value. Resentment against the so-called land grabs grew within the community. In the end, $607,846.50 was paid out by the city and a further $20,606.44 in back taxes and unpaid bills was assumed by the city. This amounted to less than $2,000 per person.

In its efforts to assist the relocation of blacks into surrounding white communities, the city assigned social workers to the project. They undertook to locate suitable housing for the dispossessed, to encourage Africville residents to begin adult education courses, and to find jobs for the unemployed.

Also of importance, many Africville residents soon discovered that the removal project undermined that sense of community they felt so strongly in Africville. Under pressure of a community breaking up, factions developed. Some of the young people, forced to move, set out for Montreal and Toronto; others felt that they could better themselves in Halifax; still others resisted the removal plans, and those who had formal title to their land clung to Africville, believing they would be lost in the city once they were separated from the community they knew.

Muriel Sparks, who ran one of the two small stores in Africville, was typical. She worried that her community church, the Seaview African United Baptist Church, would cease to function once the Africville congregation was spread all over Halifax. The church was founded in 1854 and it was more than a religious institution; it had been both the local social center and the community meeting hall of Africville for many years. While attendance at formal church services was small, demolition of the church building, which relocation would bring, became a symbol of the coming total destruction of the Africville community—a fact which increasingly aroused the wider black community, in Nova Scotia specifically and in Canada generally.

Dr. W. P. Oliver, Africville's Baptist minister, who eventually took up employment with the provincial Department of Education, was not optimistic about the future of his people:

> It's alright to be philosophical and talk about "rehabilitating" people—but what's really happening to the folk of Africville. Many of the young are simply running away. . . . The city's relocation plans are fast developing into a programme of temporary shelter for the aged . . . .

In the end protest was useless. Financial settlements were paid out and the community died. When accommodation, often in public housing projects in Halifax, became available, Africville families were relocated. In what some Africville residents felt was a final indignity, many families saw all their personal goods and furniture loaded onto yellow Halifax garbage trucks which served as vans in moving them to their new homes.

Although 16 January 1964 was cited as the date Africville "officially died," Africville was not finally buried until five years later, on 6 January 1969. That day bulldozers moved in and demolished the last house in Africville, the home of seventy-two-year-old Aaron "Pa" Miller.

In an interview with the *Halifax Mail-Star* (2 January 1970), Pa Miller revealed much of himself, his life, and his feelings at being forced to leave his home. Pa's roots in Africville trace back prior to the American Civil War. During that period his grandfather escaped slavery, settled in Africville, then left to serve Canada in the Boer War. Pa's grandfather lived to be 125 and Pa's father, a small contractor, to be 95. Pa Miller had been a coal handler and stevedore on the Halifax waterfront until he finally retired in 1965.

It was not by chance that Pa Miller was the last resident to leave Africville. He fought relocation. As Pa told the *Halifax Mail-Star* reporter, "I didn't want to leave, I was born there, got married and raised my family there. I'm getting ready to die so what the hell do I want to leave for—I liked it there." He had title to his property and refused one city offer of $12,000 for his land and a second offer of $14,000 a month later.

But Pa could not hold out much longer. His house stood on the spot where the city was prepared to lay down an access road for the new $35-million A. Murray MacKay Bridge linking Halifax to Dartmouth across the harbor. He was told that if he refused, his land would be expropriated. After arguing with city officials and delaying the move as long as possible, Pa Miller finally settled for $14,387.76 and moved into a low-rental city-owned house.

When reporter Jim Robson asked Pa Miller his opinion about the whole relocation project, he replied, "The city should never have moved the people from Africville. They should have built homes for them and given them the chance to pay for their homes . . . ."

Postscript
In 1971 a four-hundred-page report by the Dalhousie University Institute of Public Affairs was published exploring the consequences of the Africville removal project. While the report claimed the city had succeeded in its goal of demolishing Africville, the consequences prove far from a success story. The report claimed that "some black leaders have begun to suspect that relocation may be a form of race warfare" destroying the black community while claiming to be assisting individual blacks to better themselves.

Did individuals better themselves? The report says no. Most of those relocated in other parts of Halifax ended up worse off than before. They were put into homes or apartments where rents or payments often could not be met. In the mainstream of Halifax life their cost of living went up and many were forced onto welfare rolls for the first time in their lives. The retraining programs which were organized to assist Africville residents failed to produce job opportunities.

Equally important, the report noted that most relocated Africville residents missed Africville—their old surroundings, their sense of community, the closeness of neighbors whom they knew and understood. In demolishing an unsightly slum, the city had also destroyed a black community.

The Issues

• Should Africville have been demolished and Africville's residents relocated in scattered fashion throughout
Halifax?

The Decision to Destroy Africville

• Which of the following factors do you believe contributed to the decision to destroy Africville? Explain
your position.

   –a concern by Halifax City Council about the slum
     conditions existing in Africville
   –a fear by Halifax City Council of the existence of a
     solid black community on the edge of the city
   –a desire by the Halifax City Council to use the Afric-
     ville area for industrial or other profitable economic
     enterprises
   –a concern by Africville residents about the poor con-
     ditions in which they lived
   –a desire by Africville residents to break out of their
     segregated community
   –none of the above
   –a combination of the above

• What other factors can you think of which might have
contributed to the decision to demolish Africville?

• Do you agree with the plan offered by Dr. Albert Rose
to solve the Africville situation?

   –compensation for land holdings
   –resettlement in Halifax

• Even though the city council has the legal right to ex-
propriate property and plan for urban development in
the community as a whole, should it have a right to destroy a community like Africville in the process? Explain
your answer.

• Should the decision to demolish Africville have been

carried out after Africville residents overwhelmingly objected to the removal plan?

• Would it have been right for the Africville residents to refuse to cooperate with the decision of a democratically elected municipal government? Why or why not?

Analogy

Africville is not the only recent case where a small community was destroyed by government decision. In Newfoundland, little isolated outport fishing villages have survived for generations through periods of both hardship and prosperity. However, in more recent years, these communities have lagged far behind larger Newfoundland population centers in public services, health care, and educational facilities. In addition, the government of Newfoundland claimed that the declining fishing economy of these outport villages was not strong enough to justify the costs of improvements necessary to raise the standard of living in outports to equal that elsewhere in the province.

As a result the government decided that in one outport village after another the local population should be moved to larger centers. Over the objections of local residents a series of them were cut off from support and public services. Instead, financial assistance was given to each village to assist in its relocation.

After a few outport villages had been relocated, the program was judged to be largely a failure, a fact which even Newfoundland's Premier Frank Moores has now admitted. The sense of community spirit which held outport villages together and gave them their special flavor was destroyed. Once the people were moved to larger population centers, close family ties began to break. Employment which suited the fishing folk was difficult to find in cities and what was found proved unsatisfactory.

26

Criticism of the relocation project grew and eventually forced the government to scale down the scheme. Ultimately only those families or individuals who request assistance to relocate elsewhere in Newfoundland are given aid. No more outport villages will be relocated en masse. Those outport villages requiring financial assistance will be granted provincial aid. Those villages already relocated are lost forever.

• Do you believe that the outport villages should be allowed to survive so long as the local residents want them to do so?

• Should they survive only so long as they are self-supporting and, therefore, not an expense to the rest of the province's taxpayers?

• Should they receive financial assistance to survive even if it will cost the provincial taxpayer a lot of money? Why or why not?

• How is the situation of Newfoundland outport villages similar to or different from the situation of Africville and its removal project?

• Should Africville have been given financial assistance in order to help it survive? Explain your answer.

Africville: Community or Ghetto?
• Do you believe Africville was a black community or a black ghetto in Halifax?

• Was it right for Africville blacks to press for their continued existence segregated from the surrounding white city?

• What do you believe is more important—the right of a group to exist separately if it chooses, even if it may upset the rest of the city, or the need to integrate all groups in the city into one large community? Discuss your answer.

• Can you think of other possible options?

• Is there any real difference between segregation when it is self-imposed by blacks and when it is forced by the surrounding whites? If so, how?

• What do you believe are the advantages of any racial, religious, or language group living separately from other groups? What are the disadvantages?

• Can different groups of people be forced to live together? Should they be forced to live together? Is it wrong for different groups not to want to live together? Why or why not?

• Who should decide whether different groups should live together or apart? Explain your choice or choices.
  –the majority group
  –the government
  –each individual
  –an outside expert

• Would it have been easier for the all-black community of Africville to remain apart if it were a wealthy community instead of a slum? Do you believe that the community would have been forced to relocate into white Halifax if it had been a wealthy community?

• If Africville were a wealthy black community, do you believe the Halifax City Council would have demolished a neighboring white community and forced its relocation in Africville? Why or why not?

• If Africville's population had to be relocated because Africville was a slum in such poor condition that it could not be salvaged, would it have been just to relocate Africville residents *together* in a more prosperous area of Halifax?

• How do you think the rest of the Halifax community would have responded to the relocation of the Africville community all together in another area of Halifax?

• What would have been the advantages or disadvantages of such a move, if it were possible?

Parallel Situation

In 1967 Toronto's new multimillion-dollar city hall and plaza opened where much of the city's old Chinatown once stood. The few Chinese stores and restaurants that remained were located on prime commercial land desired by developers and land speculators.

The Chinese community became alarmed when rumors started to circulate of further expropriation and the possible widening of Dundas Street running through the heart of their community. There was nowhere else, they argued, that they could relocate at reasonable prices in the downtown area. A group of young articulate men in the Chinese community organized themselves to fight for their community's survival.

In 1969 they formed a "Save Chinatown Committee." A brief was written to present to the city's Building and Development meeting on April 14. The purpose of the brief was threefold: to voice the views of the Chinese community about the future of Chinatown; to explain the implications of present city planning policies that might actually lead to the complete elimination of Chinatown; and to urge the city to consult with the leaders of the Chinese community in planning any future development of the Chinatown area. When the crisis was averted the committee dissolved, but its leaders remained alert to the very shaky situation facing Chinatown.

The following year Toronto Chinese business and community leaders held a two-day conference on the state of the Chinese community. They brought together many people interested in the needs of the community in order to discuss common problems and how they could improve their lines of communication with city officials and one another.

Mrs. Jean Lumb, a community worker and committee member, made a convincing case for the need to preserve older areas of Chinatown. Although only a third of Toronto's approximately 14,000 Chinese still lived in

Chinatown and the surrounding area, new Chinese immigrants arrived every year needing a place to begin life in Canada, "a place where they can be among their own people and hear their own language spoken."

Mrs. Lumb denied that Chinatown was a ghetto, as some critics claimed. To Chinese Canadians it was a place to live, shop, eat, and feel at home. It was a place where they could keep up their ties with the past while they became part of the fabric of Canadian society.

Although the committee acknowledged that the older areas of Chinatown were then somewhat rundown and shabby, they asked City Hall for a chance to improve it. If the city would give them assurances that zoning laws would not be changed to favor high-rise hotel and apartment developers, Chinese merchants and property owners would no longer be afraid to improve their property. A repainted and generally renovated Chinatown would be a tourist attraction, an asset to the city as well as to the Chinese community.

In March 1971 events seemed to move against the continued existence of Chinatown. City council approved changing the downtown core density regulations to permit the spread of high-rise offices and apartments, in a westward direction from University Avenue to include McCaul Street, a predominantly low-cost Chinese residential area close to the remaining commercial district of Chinatown. A development known as Windlass presented a plan of high-rise apartments and a shopping center for McCaul street whose rents would be far beyond the income of the many Chinese people living in the area. The leaders of the Chinese community asked for a freeze on all rezoning regulations until an in-depth study of the area and its needs could be made.

Late in the fall of 1972 the municipal elections returned a new mayor and city council to office. Many of the new aldermen had run on a platform that favored retaining the downtown area of the city without a great deal of additional development. The new council shelved plans to widen Dundas Street for at least another year until the implications could be studied in further detail. The Windlass corporation was forced to redesign and submit new plans to City Hall. This time they presented a scheme of low-rise apartments that would include 20 percent subsidized housing, likely to be filled by local Chinese residents.

The future of Toronto's old Chinatown area is far from secure. However, the new climate at City Hall, the growing economic and political power of the Toronto Chinese community, and their watchfulness increase their chances for survival. In the meantime, the Toronto Chinese community and its Chinatown slowly began to drift westward on its own. While the older areas of Chinatown still required protection against developers, new areas of Chinese population and business concentration have begun to crop up to the immediate west of old Chinatown, along Dundas and north on Spadina Avenue, where pressure from high-rise and commercial developers was far less.

Postscript
In July 1975, municipal authorities decided not to widen Dundas Street.

• Were Toronto municipal authorities justified in uprooting the local Chinese community in order to promote urban development?

• Should such neighborhoods be preserved?

• Should Chinatown be preserved if it stands in the way of:
  —a low-rental housing development that would house far more people than housing conditions presently allow?
  —a hotel shopping complex that would attract tourists and provide jobs for local residents?

31

–expansion of the nearby university, which is pressed for space?

–creation of a giant park in a city pressed for park land?

–completion of a major highway expansion?

• In your opinion what difference would it make if the following factors, true for Toronto's Chinatown, would or could be applied to the case of Africville? Give your reasons.

–a much larger population in both Halifax and Africville

–Africville being in the center of the city instead of on the edge of the city

–a large number of black merchants and professionals living in Africville or Halifax

–an anti-development Halifax city council

–a greater number of politically astute and active members of the black community

• How is the situation described in Toronto's Chinatown the same or different from Halifax's Africville?

3

Housing and
Discrimination

On 10 December 1963, twenty-two-year-old Carl McKay
found a small classified advertisement in a Toronto newspaper offering a three-room flat with private bath and
kitchen for rent in the city's west end. McKay telephoned
the number given in the advertisement and was told that
the flat was not yet rented. The following day McKay
and another young man who planned to be McKay's
roommate went to seee the flat in a three-storey private
house on Indian Road.

They met disappointment. As they stood at the door-
way of the house they were told by the owner, Kenneth
S. Bell, that the advertised flat had already been rented.

McKay was not convinced. Sensing that Bell might not
be telling the truth, McKay requested that a friend,
Nancy Sharp, inquire about the same flat later that very
day. She was informed by Bell that the apartment was
still vacant.

McKay believed that the reason he had been wrongly
told the flat was rented was on account of his race. Mc-
Kay was black. As far as he was concerned, Bell's refusal to rent the flat was racial discrimination. In a letter

to the Ontario Human Rights Commission McKay explained, "I am a Black man from Jamaica and feel that my failure to obtain accommodation was determined by factors of race, color and place of origin."

If, as he claimed, McKay had been discriminated against in his attempt to rent an apartment on account of his race, the law seemed clear enough in prohibiting discrimination. Section 3 of the Ontario Human Rights Code 1961–62 states, in part, that

> No person, directly or indirectly, alone or with another, by himself or by the interposition of another, shall, (a) deny to any person or class of persons occupancy of any commercial unit or self-contained dwelling unit ... because of the race, creed, colour, nationality, ancestry or place of origin of such person or class of persons.

McKay was not about to let what he felt to be racial discrimination pass lightly. He demanded that the Ontario Human Rights Commission take action against Bell under section 3 of the Code.

The Ontario Human Rights Commission, a provincial government agency which operates within the Ministry of Labour, is authorized to investigate complaints by persons who, like Carl McKay, claim that their rights under the Ontario Human Rights Code have been violated. In accord with the current procedure, if the complaint proved correct or seemed justified, the Commission tried to arrange for a settlement. If the Commission failed to achieve a satisfactory settlement, it could organize a board of inquiry on the authority of the Minister of Labour. The board would attempt to establish the exact facts of the case and make a recommendation for settlement. Failing a settlement based on these recommendations, the Commission, as a last resort, could proceed into a court action against the person thought to have violated the Code.

Carl McKay's complaint routinely followed this standard procedure. The final outcome, however, was to prove far from satisfactory to McKay. The alleged violation of McKay's rights soon got lost in a maze of legal maneuvers. In the end it was Kenneth Bell, the home owner, who emerged to some as the defender of human rights; Carl McKay and the problem he had in finding a place to live in a white community would be forgotten. It was the Ontario Human Rights Commission who would virtually be put on trial.

This strange turnabout began less than a month after Bell refused to allow McKay to rent the Indian Road flat. On 2 January 1964 the Commission notified Bell that it had looked carefully into McKay's charges of racial discrimination. After carrying out what it called a "thorough investigation" of McKay's complaint, the Commission advised Bell that it "had found sufficient evidence supporting Mr. McKay's allegations of discrimination to warrant further involvement of the Commission in this matter." The Commission requested a meeting with Bell to "discuss possible terms of settlement and conciliation." In a case such as this, terms might include a written expression of apology to McKay, an offer of the next available accommodation, and payment of possible financial costs resulting from any inconvenience Bell's refusal had caused McKay.

Bell requested assistance from his lawyer, William C. Cuttell, in dealing with the Commission. Cuttell in turn informed the Commission that his client would not make a settlement without a just court hearing and, furthermore, that Bell denied violating any part of the Ontario Human Rights Code. Cuttell explained to the Commission that if it felt Bell had indeed violated the law, the Commission should take Bell to court.

Rather than go to court, which was normally its last resort, the Commission advised Bell that a board of inquiry had been appointed to conduct public hearings into

McKay's complaint of racial discrimination. The board was to investigate and advise the Commission what steps should then be taken, perhaps including a possible move into the courts. Walter Tarnopolsky, then Dean of Windsor University Law School, was appointed chairman of the board of inquiry. Bell was further advised that his presence at the board's meeting was mandatory.

Bell objected to a board hearing. Working through his lawyer, Bell appealed directly to the Ontario Minister of Labour, who is responsible for the Human Rights Commission. Bell requested that the board be disbanded. While he still claimed he had violated no law, Bell again argued that if the Commission felt a law had been broken it should take him to court, not set up a board of inquiry.

The request was denied. The board of inquiry was established. The board met in the provincial Parliament Buildings at Queen's Park in downtown Toronto on 21 April 1969. Bell's lawyer argued that Bell had violated no law and therefore the board had no jurisdiction in this case. He again requested that the board disband or immediately advise the Commission to go to court against Mr. Bell. The board refused to disband. It claimed it did have jurisdiction to hold public hearings into the alleged case of discrimination against Carl McKay. If the board found that a settlement could not be reached then it might recommend going to court, but not before.

If the Commission would not disband its board of inquiry and go to court against Bell, Bell was quite prepared to go to court himself. In the Ontario Supreme Court, Bell sought an injunction to stop the Commission and its board of inquiry from continuing its investigation. In what was quickly to become a seesaw court battle, the problems encountered by McKay in attempting to rent a flat seemingly got lost.

In court, Bell requested an injunction to stop the board's deliberations on the grounds that the board, indeed the Commission itself, had no jurisdiction in this

36

case because he had violated no law. Rather Bell claimed the Commission's procedures violated his rights. If the Commission felt that there had been a violation of the law, Bell again argued, he should be tried in a court of law, not before a board of inquiry.

In an affidavit to the court, complete with photographs, Bell described both the particular flat in question and the meeting with McKay at the time when he inquired about the flat. As Bell explained it, there had been no racial discrimination involved in the rejection of McKay and his friend. "I did not refuse to rent to the negroes because they were negroes but because they were too young and appeared to be students, and I do not want young men or students as tenants, particularly because the flat is not separate from my living quarters and is not self-contained."

Although he denied that there had been any racially motivated intent on his part, Bell did admit to the court that he had indeed lied when he told McKay the flat had already been rented. However, his lie was not intended to be malicious, but as he explained to the court, for convenience ". . . it is the simplest method and avoids discussion and argument."

Bell not only denied any racial discrimination on his part, but he also challenged the right of the Ontario Human Rights Commission to investigate this particular incident, even if racial discrimination had been involved. Bell contended that the flat on Indian Road was not "self-contained." As he reminded the court, the Ontario Human Rights Code 1961–62 limits the Commission to take action only in cases of discrimination in a "commercial unit of self-contained dwelling." Since his flat was not "self-contained," he argued, the Commission had no right to look into the affair.

Ontario Supreme Court
Mr. Justice Charles Stewart of the Ontario Supreme

37

Court examined the photographs of the Indian Road flat. It was clear from the photographs that tenants would have to enter through the front door of the house and climb an open stairway to the second and third floors to reach the advertised flat.

Mr. Justice Stewart agreed with Bell that the flat was not "self-contained" and thus not covered by the Act. According to Mr. Justice Stewart the Commission must have defined "self-contained" unit in an unusual way to give itself jurisdiction in the case; failing that, the Commission had not really made a thorough enough inquiry as to the nature of the accommodations being advertised by Mr. Bell. Since it was obvious that the flat in question was not "self-contained," neither the Human Rights Commission nor any board of inquiry it set up had any jurisdiction to deal with the matter. Mr. Justice Stewart added, "It is equally obvious that before any board of inquiry had been appointed, the Commission had already made up its mind. Had this house been divided into self-contained apartments, the Act would apply and discrimination would be prohibited." But this was not the case. Mr. Justice Stewart reminded the Commission that the Act was never intended to deprive a man of his own choice of tenants when the rooms in question are unseparated from the remainder of the house.

Mr. Justice Stewart then turned his attention to the powers of the Commission. According to Bell's lawyer, William Cuttell, section 28 of the Labour Relations Act, which had set up the Commission, gave the Commission the right to "investigate," and nothing else. Cuttell deemed it "a perversion of that right" to conduct an investigation by setting up a board of inquiry when sufficient evidence about the complaint was already in hand. Certainly, he pointed out, if the Commission was only to investigate, the board of inquiry had no power to recommend any settlement without a court hearing. Without such a court hearing Bell would have no opportunity of finding out what evidence could be brought against him.

Cuttell also pointed out that it was improper to suggest that a violation of the Human Rights Code, if one had indeed been committed, could be made right by a simple payment of compensation money or other methods of settlement. That is, there was nothing in the Code which gave the Commission the right to establish a settlement; that, Cuttell argued, was the job of the courts.

Once again Mr. Justice Stewart agreed with Bell. Nowhere throughout the normal process of inquiry by the Commission was a citizen allowed to have a "recognized court presided over by a provincial judge make a finding on the law and its merits unless the minister (of Labour) gives leave." Accordingly Mr. Justice Stewart ordered an injunction to stop the board of inquiry. He summed up the case and his reasons for intervention as follows:

> It is equally important that the rights of a middle-aged white Canadian homeowner be protected as those of a young black Jamaican tenant. Neither more important or less important. Equally. And perhaps it is time that this was made clear.

Ontario Court of Appeal
As is often customary where an important point of law is at stake, the case was appealed to a higher court. The Crown Attorney, acting for the Commission, called for a hearing in the Ontario Court of Appeal. On 20 November 1969, Mr. Justice Bora Laskin, with the support of the four fellow Appeal Court judges, reversed the Stewart decision. The Appeal Court judgment stated that Mr. Justice Stewart was wrong in ruling that the board of inquiry had no jurisdiction before the inquiry had heard the evidence. It would, Mr. Justice Laskin argued, be part of the duty of the board of inquiry set up by the Commission to decide whether the flat in question was a self-contained unit. In the end, therefore, the board itself

could have decided whether it had jurisdiction or not. If the board of inquiry found the flat was not "self-contained" it could call off the inquiry on its own. No injunction was necessary.

Supreme Court of Canada
Bell took his case to the Supreme Court of Canada. Two years later on 1 February 1971 the Supreme Court reversed the decision of the Ontario Court of Appeal and in a 5 to 2 decision agreed with the original decision of Mr. Justice Stewart. The court ruled for Bell.

The Supreme Court of Canada claimed that the accommodation was not covered by the code because the accommodation was not "self-contained." In his nineteen-page judgment Mr. Justice Ronald Martland stated, "In my opinion, the premises leased by the appellant (Mr. Bell) in his upstairs floors may well be dwelling units but they were not self-contained dwelling units." The main issue in the case, according to Mr. Justice Martland, was whether the Supreme Court of Ontario has the power to prevent the Ontario Human Rights Commission from proceeding with investigation of a complaint of discrimination which does not fall within the scope of the Ontario Human Rights Code. The Supreme Court held that such an investigation could be prevented.

A Supreme Court majority found that Mr. Bell was entitled to seek an order of prohibition, an injunction, against a board of inquiry and that Mr. Justice Stewart of the Ontario Supreme Court was entitled to grant it. If the "dwelling unit" is not "self-contained" there could be no investigation or board of inquiry. To quote the judgment:

> The powers given to a board of inquiry are to enable it to determine whether or not there has been discrimination in respect of matters within the scope of the Act (*The Ontario Human Rights Code, 1961–62*). It has no power to deal with alleged discrimination in matters

not within the purview of the act or to make recommendations with respect thereto.

The case had dragged on for more than two years and Bell had finally won. It was decided that the Ontario Human Rights Commission went beyond its powers in pursuing its investigation of McKay's claim that he had been discriminated against on account of race. The flat in question was not "a self-contained dwelling unit." Bell, or any other landlord, could, if he so pleased, freely discriminate on account of race or any other grounds in choosing tenants in such an apartment.

In an editorial on 4 January 1971 the *Toronto Globe and Mail* praised Bell for standing up to the Commission, refusing to give in to the Commission's settlement proposals, and finally emerging victorious from the highest court in the land. As the *Toronto Globe and Mail* explained, "Had Mr. Bell not been a stubborn man determined not to succumb to bureaucratic pressure, he would have signed whatever confession the commission officials put in front of him. . . . When a person's reputation in the community is at stake, it takes courage to refuse."

Neither the newspaper nor the courts asked whether Carl McKay eventually found a place to live.

Postcript
As a result, in part, of the Supreme Court ruling, changes were made in the Ontario Human Rights Code legislation and Commission procedures. The term "self-contained" was removed from the legislation. In its place it was set down that the Commission should have jurisdiction in all cases of discrimination in housing except where the owner of the accommodation and his family share kitchen and washroom facilities with the tenant. With this change, there would be no further doubts about flats like the one Bell had for rent. They are now covered by the Code.

In 1972 the role of the board of inquiry also changed. Whereas a board of inquiry was previously required to report back to the Commission for further action, a board of inquiry is not now dependent on the Human Rights Commission. Once established by the Minister of Labour, the board has the power to carry forward its own recommendations for a settlement or go to court.

Had McKay's case come before the Ontario Human Rights Commission today, it is less likely that Bell would have been able to stop the proceedings.

The Issues

• Should Kenneth Bell have had the right to refuse to rent to Carl McKay?

McKay versus Bell

• Bell told McKay that the flat was already rented when this was not true. Knowing this, what is your opinion on each of the following:

–Why did Bell lie?

–Do you think he was justified?

–If Bell had told McKay that the flat was still available but that he was only going to rent it to married or mature persons do you think that would have avoided the difficulties which followed?

–If you were McKay, would you have believed Bell if you were told the flat was already rented? Why?

–If you were McKay, would you have believed Bell if you were told the flat would only be rented to mature or married persons?

–If McKay were white instead of black do you think he would have believed that the flat was already rented?

• Since Bell said he was only interested in renting to mature or married people would it have been better to include this fact in his newspaper advertisement?

• Do you believe it was reasonable for Bell to want only mature or married persons as tenants?

• Should Bell have a right to discriminate on the basis of age?

• Since McKay felt he was discriminated against on account of his race, he went to the Ontario Human Rights Commission. Can you think of anything different that you would have done?

• What do you think of the following alternatives that McKay could have chosen once he found out the flat was not really rented?
  – go back to Bell and ask him to explain why he lied
  – picket Bell's house until the flat was offered
  – forget the whole thing and look for a flat in another neighborhood

Human Rights Commission
• Do you believe that agencies like the Ontario Human Rights Commission are necessary across Canada?

• If a person believes that he has been discriminated against and this discrimination is outlawed by law, should he go to the Human Rights Commission instead of the police? Should violation of human rights be treated differently from violation of other laws?

• In other areas of law, if a person is accused of breaking the law, he goes on trial. Why do you think the Human Rights Commission only took cases to court if other attempts to settle the issue failed? Should persons violating the Human Rights Code be treated differently from persons who violate other laws?

• Was Bell right in demanding a court hearing?

• If he settled with McKay out of court, wouldn't Bell

43

be accepting some kind of punishment for a crime for which there had been no trial?

Analogy 1

In most areas of Canada if a person gets a parking ticket two options are open. If the person chooses to plead guilty to the violation outlined on the ticket it is possible to pay the fine demanded on the parking ticket by mail or at a local payment office. By doing this the person is pleading guilty to the parking violation. If a person decides that he would rather go to court than plead guilty to the violation, this option is also open. In the court his guilt must be proven and usually the officer who gave the parking ticket is present to explain why the ticket was issued. The person who received the ticket can speak in his own defense or bring witnesses.

• Do you think that something as small as parking tickets needs to be settled in court?

• If a person will lose a day's salary by going to court or must travel a great distance to get to court that person might be tempted to plead guilty, pay the fine, and save himself the problem of going to court even though he feels he is innocent. Is this fair?

• If a person feels he did not violate a law, like the Ontario Human Rights Code, but that there might be too much cost, bad publicity, or time lost by going to court, should he agree to a settlement organized by the Human Rights Commission?
  –Is this fair?
  –Should all cases be forced to go to court?

• Who should decide if a settlement outside of court is fair? Who should decide if a court case is needed?
  –the person accused of violating the law
  –the person discriminated against
  –the Human Rights Commission
  –the courts

44

–the government
–an independent board of inquiry
–all or any of the above

• Who should decide if the Human Rights Code has been violated in the first place?
    –the person discriminated against
    –the Human Rights Commission
    –the courts
    –the government
    –an independent board of inquiry
    –the police
    –all or any of the above

The Final Decision

• After a long court battle it was finally decided that Bell's flat was not "self-contained" and, therefore, not covered by the Ontario Human Rights Code 1961–62. Bell could select or reject anyone who applied for the flat for any reason he wanted.
    –Do you believe this was a good decision?
    –Do you believe the decision would have been different if the complaint against Bell had been made by a mature married black couple instead of by McKay? Why or why not?

• Since the court's decision, the law has been changed. Now the law covers all housing except in a case where a landlord shares kitchen or washroom facilities with his tenant.
    –Do you believe the changes in the law were necessary?
    –How do you think this would have changed the outcome of the Bell and McKay case if it had been the law at the time?

The Rights of the Landlord

• We have all heard people say that "A man's house is

his castle." What do you think this means? Do you agree?

• If a man owns his own home, do you believe that the government or anyone else should tell him what he must do or not do in his own house?

• Which of the following regulations affecting home owners in various parts of Canada do you believe are justified and which are not? Explain your answer in each case.

-Homeowners must clear snow from sidewalks in front of their property within twelve hours.
-Homeowners shall not cut down a tree on their property without a permit.
-Homeowners must obtain a permit before making improvements in their homes.
-No more than two children should be allowed to sleep in a single room.
-No business should operate from a private home.

• Should the government make laws which force landlords to rent space to persons they do not want to have in their homes?

-Does government legislation force individuals to live together?

• Bell claimed that he did not discriminate on account of race but because McKay was a single young man and Bell wanted only mature or married tenants. Do you believe that age discrimination is justified any more than discrimination on the basis of race, sex, religion, nationality, or place of origin?

• Which of the following do you feel is discriminatory and should be outlawed and which is not? Explain your answer.

-refusal to rent to families with children
-refusal to rent to persons with pets
-refusal to rent to paroled criminals

    —refusal to rent to persons with a criminal record
    —refusal to rent to persons recently released from
      mental institutions

  • Are there times when discrimination may be justified?
Can you think of any such cases?

Selling Property
  • If a person sells a house and moves out of the neighborhood, the seller leaves behind a new homeowner. Do
you believe that the seller's neighbors should have any
direct influence on deciding who should buy the house
and move into the neighborhood?

Analogy 2
In the past, some neighborhoods in Canadian and American cities were kept exclusively for one group. It was not
uncommon for an informal agreement called *restrictive
covenant* to exist between neighbors that they would not
sell to persons of another religion or race. Sometimes
these covenants were actually put into the original terms
of sale so that the homeowner who wanted to sell his
property could sell only to a member of the acceptable
group. Any new owner agreed that if he ever sold the
property, he would also sell it only to a member of the
acceptable group.
    Courts have now ruled that these agreements are
neither valid nor binding.

Analogy 3
Some real-estate men have been accused of a practice
called *blockbusting*. There are several variations of blockbusting but often it goes as follows: when a house goes
up for sale in an all-white neighborhood a real-estate
agent arranges for a black family to buy or rent the
house. The real-estate agent then goes from door to door
in the neighborhood warning local home owners that
unless they sell their homes and move fast they will be

caught in a black neighborhood. Playing on racial fear, he talks about a fall in the value of local property, a decline in the quality of education, and increased crime in the streets.

As frightened whites sell out, other blacks move into the neighborhood which, in turn, frightens still more whites. As the process escalates the real-estate man makes a big profit from the quick turnover in property ownership.

• Unless agreements on restricting the sale of homes to members of the group are kept, can blockbusting be stopped?

• Do you believe that blockbusting should be stopped? Should it be illegal? Why or why not?

• If a man decides to sell his house, should it be any concern of his who the new owner might be so long as the new owner can pay for the property he has purchased?

• Does a seller have any responsibility to his old neighbors? If so, should it be covered by law?

• Do you believe that neighborhoods should have some rights to regulate who moves in or out of the neighborhood? How could such arrangements be regulated?

• Is race or religion of new neighbors grounds for concern?

Associations
• Laws have prohibited most forms of discrimination which may have existed in employment, schools, housing, and public services. Do you believe that private clubs and associations should also be prevented from discrimination on account of race, religion, sex, nationality, or place of national origin?

• If you were on the membership committee for each of the following clubs or associations what would you do about the following applications? Whom would you admit? Whom would you exclude? Give your reasons in each case.

–a white businessman applies to join a black businessmen's association
–a woman applies to join the town YMCA which is closer to her home than the YWCA
–a girl applies to join the Boy Scouts
–a boy applies to join the Girl Guides
–an American wishes to join the Canadian Legion
–a high-school teacher applies to join the Student Athletic Society

• If you decided to reject any of these applications do you believe that the rejected applicant could argue that there had been discrimination on account of race, religion, sex, nationality, or place of origin?

• How could you explain a rejection so that the rejected person would believe that discrimination had not taken place?

• Is discrimination on the basis of race, religion, sex, nationality, or place of origin ever justified in clubs or associations?

• What is to prevent people who wish to discriminate from forming clubs to disguise discrimination?

Analogy 4
Outside of Washington, D.C., an apartment house was built with an attached recreation center. Rather than rent an apartment in the complex, persons were invited to join an athletic club which offered an apartment as part of the membership. Thus, instead of paying rent, residents of the apartment paid dues. Blacks were not invited to become members of the club. As a result the club was used to bypass the laws against discrimination in housing.

• Do you think that this club should be considered a club

under the law? Why or why not?

• This case was taken to court. Do you think this type of club was found to be legal or illegal? Explain your answer.

4

A Letter from Fort St. James

Author's Note

The research which goes into the preparation of Canadian Public Issues units such as *Issues in Cultural Diversity* brings the authors into contact with many different types of research sources. These often include newspaper reports, court records, government publications, and interviews with individuals involved in the specific case under investigation. When persons who might act as a source of information live some distance from the authors, a letter is usually sent requesting information.

What follows is the answer to such a research request letter. It deals with the tension between immigrants from India/Pakistan and the native people in central and northern British Columbia. Normally any information gathered in this way from knowledgeable individuals is used in conjunction with other collected sources. The authors then use all material collected on the topic to prepare the case stories used in each unit. In this instance the authors have decided to make an exception. We publish this letter on its own rather than use it as one source in preparing our own outline of the case.

The authors think that while the letter cannot pretend to be neutral (and does not reflect the views of the authors), it does specifically outline a delicate situation with a degree of detail and feeling which might be useful for readers of this unit to consider. The authors trust that the letter will be read in this light.

On 26 September 1973 the authors wrote Ruth M. Hallock, editor of the *Caledonia Courier* in Fort St. James, British Columbia, requesting detailed information on reported street fights between native people and immigrants in the Fort St. James area then being mentioned in the media. What follows is Ruth Hallock's reply dated 3 October 1973.

CALEDONIA COURIER
"Answering the Call of the North"

C. G. (Bud) Hallock   P.O. Box 108,
Publisher   Fort St. James, B.C.

Ruth M. Hallock
Editor

October 3, 1973

Ms. Lee Palmer,
Research Officer,
Ontario Institute for Studies in Education,
252 Bloor Street West,
Toronto 5, Ontario, Canada.

Dear Ms. Palmer:

In reply to your letter of September 26th, I must confess I am somewhat at a loss as to where to begin.

The Fort St. James incident last summer was not something that just happened overnight. In my opinion it really had nothing to do with racism or skin colour or creed or language barriers or any of those things. Rather it had its origins in complete ignorance, and lack of civilized self-control on the part of people who have lived here for well over a century in continuing generations.

As I stated in the article your letter makes reference to—the ignition for deep-rooted habits of stupidity on the part of participants in the summer incident stemmed from liquor, which is a very strong source of trouble in this community as in many other northern communities.

To put it more bluntly—in Fort St. James there are a lot of idle people, many of whom are of Canadian Indian extraction. They live on a Reserve located within the natural boundaries of the village and only a short walking distance from the town's only beer parlour. A few extra steps will get them to the town's only Government Liquor Store. They seem to have money in their pockets despite the fact that only a small percentage of them work in local industry. The source of this money is debatable. Perhaps some of it comes from furs taken from almost aboriginal trapping areas. Perhaps some of it comes from public dole. In any case, the Canadian Indian population of Fort St. James which consists of about 600 on the "in town" Necoslie Reserve and another 400 from the Tachie Reserve, eighteen miles west, seems well enough heeled to be able to buy continuing large quantities of wine and beer whenever boredom sets in. It seems to set in with mounting frequency as the local beer parlour is, on any day of the week, found to be two thirds occupied by people of Canadian Indian extraction. The Government Liquor Store, which opens at ten every morning, always has a waiting line-up of at least five people, generally native Indians, when the doors are unlocked. Oddly enough, I have been picking up my mail daily for the past five years at the local Post Office, next to the Liquor Store, usually at 9:30 or 9:45 a.m. and I can honestly state that I have not yet seen one day when there is not someone waiting for the Liquor Store to open. Quite often, the people waiting there are already drunked up from an all night drinking session, and I suppose are anxious to get more supplies.

Perhaps I should hastily insert something here to deter any idea you might form that I am perhaps radically opposed to drinking. I am not averse to taking on a skinful myself once in a while—and in fact, have been known to do so. However, I suppose I simply do not have sufficient idle time on my hands to make boozing my life's career.

I am giving you a general outline of the drinking problems that exist in this community, and that have apparently existed for well over a hundred years—a problem that began when the Northwest Company fur traders first came into the area and began to get Indian women drunk in order to lure them into more extenuating practices. In fact our history shows that when first confronted with a display of drunkenness on the part of white men (during a New Year's Day celebration at the (then) Hudson's Bay fur trading post) the Indians were terrified and actually ran into the woods to hide. Gradually they came to know the effects of booze, and, unfortunately I suppose, began to lean on it more and more to offset boredom, poverty, frustration and all the other things that come to try the human race.

Today in Fort St. James, it is not uncommon for a small Indian child to actually look forward to the day when he reaches legal age so that he might join with his friends in the local beer parlour. (E.G.: Six months ago I attended a special Cub Scout tour of the RCMP Detachment and one of the young tads taking part in the tour was quite taken with the breathalizer unit. He was a member of a local Indian family. He commented, "Gee I can hardly wait til I grow up and then I can get drunk and have one of those tests on me." The others laughed of course, but damn it, I couldn't, because the kid just

MIGHT end up like so many of those before him.)

Drunkenness is a common sight here. There is not one day of the week when you do not see at least one drunk staggering down the main drag, or slumped over in an alleyway sleeping it off. In winter, drunks often die of exposure. At least I would consider three deaths annually to be "often". That figure taken over an average of the past thirty years.

I make no bones about it—the drunkenness is largely a Canadian Indian problem. Certainly the white race has its drinking problems too, but there are churches here, and there are community activities that are worthwhile, and there is a general good standard of living on the part of the white populace and "off-Reserve" Indian. I hate like fury to separate the two entities, because I personally live in a "total community concept"—one in which there are people of many racial derivations and I try to treat everyone the same regardless of his colour or his education or his creed. Perhaps because I like "people". I have in fact many, many friends of Canadian Indian extraction and am beginning to acquire friends of East Indian extraction as they arrive and settle in the community.

The East Indian people began arriving about six years ago when a local sawmill and veneer plant opened here. At that time a Vancouver man was quite active in assisting East Indian people with job placement and immigration. He worked hand in hand with the local mill to provide labourers as they were required. Because many of the East Indian people were anxious to get a new start in a new country, they accepted labourers' jobs despite the fact that in many instances they were actually skilled workers or even professionals in their original homeland.

At the outset, most of the East Indian people coming to the Fort were single men, and because of language difficulties they tended to group together. They sought out living accommodation in ghetto-like clusters and did their shopping in groups, with one official spokesman doing the talking while the others simply stood back and observed.

The townspeople generally accepted the East Indians as a new segment of the local social structure, but the fact that they travelled in groups seemed to have a deleterious effect on their stature in the community. It was commonplace to hear complaints from trades people for example, regarding the inbred bartering habits of the East Indian man. He found it difficult to accept set prices for individual items and constantly tried to barter rather than straight trade. This of course was merely a matter of adjustment, but unfortunately the die was cast and the first difference was struck. The East Indian found it hard to adjust to our climate and to our eating habits. He complained bitterly about the cold, in temperatures that were naturally acceptable to those of us who have lived in this area for generations. He sought and insisted upon specialized spice foods, and merchants eventually began to stock such items in quantity. He wore his native costume, complete with turban and turned up toes, and generally attracted attention in this manner.

Complaints began to circulate from landlords in the community, that when premises were rented to East Indian people, they suffered indestructible permeation of strong spice cooking odours. It became difficult for East Indian men to find living accommodation, and they were forced even more into the ghetto-like habits in order to survive. They purchased some houses on a shared ownership basis, and loaded up the available space with people. Fear began to germinate amongst them and their walking groups increased in size. Before long the nasty term, "hindhu" began to rear its head in the town. Basically it does not apply to East Indians as a whole but is a religion. However, ignorance on the part of other townspeople, failed to point this up, and the term became almost general in reference. In fact, I had a devil of a time breaking my 12 year old and 14 year old of the stupid terminology, which they used indiscriminately in reference to anything unpleasant or awesome. (You'll be happy to know I finally succeeded—but not without threat of bodily harm!)

An enterprising, though sometimes ethically questionable businessman in town (white), built a slap-dash two storey frame structure and labelled it a motel. Charging rents of upwards of $130.00 a month for a one bedroom unit, he threw it open to East Indian men and the place, strategically located right downtown on the main drag, became commonly known as the "Hindhu Hotel" or the "Pakistani Palace". Today it stands still in use in this capacity, in trouble with Civic authorities due to overcrowding and consequent health hazards, and is in fact the subject of a Court case—but it is still totally occupied by East Indian men, all of whom are sawmill employees, all of whom walk forth in groups, or drive in caravans, and many of whom speak no English.

Gradually many of the East Indian men began to bring their wives and families here. They purchased homes and their children started school. Special classes in English for New Canadians were started to assist them with language problems where they existed. In the schools, only up to elementary as we have no senior secondary facilities here, a natural response to a new classmate is usually one of indifference. Not so here. When an East Indian child starts school he has a strike against him already. He becomes not just a new "kid in our class"— but unfortunately "a new 'hindhu' in our class". It is a bad scene, and one I personally deplore, but have not been able to solve in my own meagre mind.

Now—for the "racist" incidents. To go back to the idle, heavy drinking Canadian Indians. Almost historically the Carrier has been a reluctant worker. They may work diligently in a regular job for a time, and then almost habitually will "fall off the wagon", go on a week-end tear and miss a shift or two. Employers, working a tight production schedule, cannot condone such practices. The East Indian, on the other hand is an exceptionally reliable worker. He minds his own business, does his job to the best of his ability, lays off the juice and shows up for work every day—on time. It's only a common sense tactic that would find an employer showing preference to the reliable worker over the unreliable worker.

But—somewhere along the line, the preference for reliability has been misconstrued as racial preference and the Canadian Indian is quick to harp about it.

Meanwhile, back at the beer parlour, where we have a preponderance of Canadian Indian imbibers, a smattering of rough neck ignorant whites, and another smattering of just plain curiosity buffs, the East Indian groups began to make tentative entertainment sorties, and on occasion attempted to make time with some of the females in the place. The Canadian Indians, when half drunk, are great to sense fear in others and they certainly sensed it in the groups of East Indians. Using whatever excuse for a fight they could find, they would set upon the East Indian men. On one occasion an East Indian was badly battered with a length of chain and required several weeks hospitalization. When police questioned him as to the identity of his assailants he refused steadfastly to co-operate. He claimed he was afraid "they" would come back for seconds and perhaps kill him the second time around. The fear grew and the fighting (spasmodic) increased.

Last summer the street trouble started with three drunk Canadian Indians, out looking for excitement. One of them is a town "nut", in and out of jail like a yo-yo on various drinking infractions. He rolled up his belt over his fist, buckle out, and proceeded to give the men from the downtown motel, (previously mentioned) a bad time, shouting obscenities and dancing around like a bantam rooster.

The East Indian men, I suppose had finally reached the breaking point, and for a change, they retaliated. There was an exchange of cuffs, one man was cut and required minor stitching, another was slightly bruised. A good sized crowd gathered and began shouting encouragement to the side of its choice. It was a means to break the monotony of an otherwise dull, hot, summer, Saturday afternoon. It irks me to have to say that people here are the same as in any other community and will always congregate for a fight or a fire or any kind of a sensational diversion. But it's true—they do. The police were called but no arrests were made, due to lack of evidence. The fight broke up fast when someone warned of their imminent arrival on the scene. An off-duty policeman was actually on hand from the beginning and saw nothing unusual for a Saturday afternoon in Fort St. James I suppose.

There's a fair amount of brawling due to drunkenness. There's a fairly high percentage of drunken driving. There's a fair degree of promiscuity and there is a high degree of vandalism. In fact we have the only Liquor Store in Canada with iron bars across the doors—this installation prompted through a series of six smash-ins inside of eight months. The price of glass is high and insurance for breakage is unattainable here.

Heaven help me—I hope I have not painted a bleak picture of the place, that tends to give you an idea that Fort St. James is the absolute end of the world. It isn't. We have the responsible side of our society that seeks to improve recreational facilities, both for whites, Indians and all. We have a really nice community—but as I have cited (somewhat lengthily I'm afraid) we have problems due to idleness, boredom, lack of personal incentives on the part of some citizens, ignorance on the part of others, and the usual things that go to besmirch any society.

Since the East Indian portion of our society has

finally asserted itself and shown the others that no-one is going to use any East Indian for a doormat, there has been a levelling off in the feeling here. The street fights have not recurred, the rock-throwing incidents are diminishing, and the people responsible for the unfair, unprovoked attacks on our new citizens have turned tail and crawled back into relative obscurity. We have about 80 East Indian families here now, and they have a registered East Indian Association which contributes to the community both at the recreational and cultural level. We have numerous improvement programs underway by the Necoslie Indian Band Council and we have the usual efforts by the responsible white populace.

With a little bit of luck, perhaps we shall survive without anymore trouble.

Sorry for the long harangue—but it is something that takes a fair amount of explaining. Hope you find some of it useful.

Yours most respectfully,

Mrs. Ruth M. Hallock

The Issues

• Who is responsible for the intergroup tensions at Fort St. James?

The Sawmill

• Should the mill owners at Fort St. James have been obliged to employ only local workers?

• If the sawmill owners considered native people an unreliable source of workers, do you believe they were justified in bringing in Pakistani, Indian, or other employees for the mill?

• Should steps have been taken to find workers in Canada before workers from abroad were encouraged to enter Canada?

• Do you think any of the following steps should have been taken by the sawmill owners before hiring workers from foreign countries?

  –try to hire workers from other parts of Canada where unemployment was high

  –try to train native people from the local area

  –hire foreign workers for short-term contracts and have them leave Canada when Canadian workers became available

  –close the sawmill until enough Canadian workers became available to operate it at full capacity

  –move the sawmill operations to a place where workers are available

  –reduce sawmill production to suit the size of the available Canadian work force

  –automate so that less labor is needed

• How do you believe each of these actions, if tried, would affect each of the following groups in Fort St. James?

  –the East Indian community

  –the local native population

  –the established white citizens

  –the sawmill owners

  –the sawmill customers

Analogy 1

Fruit farmers in Ontario's Niagara area have a problem. Every year at harvest season they need a large number of workers to pick fruit. The work is physically hard and requires very little previous training. Yet, it must be done. Farmers claim that a large pool of Canadian laborers are unavailable, or at least unavailable at the wages that farmers can pay. If they raise wages to attract Canadian workers, farmers argue that the increased costs would soon be passed on to the fruit buyer. This could

61

soon drive fruit costs up so high that it would be cheaper to buy fruit imported from other countries. High wages could therefore destroy the Canadian fruit growing industry, or so farmers claim. Similarly, it might be possible to automate the fruit picking process, but this, too, is expensive and would have to be paid for by the fruit buyer.

In order to keep labor costs low, farmers, in cooperation with federal and provincial governments, have imported laborers from the West Indies. The harvest workers stay in small work camps with poor living standards, are paid the minimum wage or almost minimum, may have unemployment insurance and other deductions taken off their wages even though they will never be able to apply for the benefits, and are sent home when their job is done.

• Do you think that temporary laborers should be imported to pick fruit?

• Should fruit growers be forced to employ only Canadian labor?

• Do you think Canadian consumers would be willing to pay higher prices for fruit to enable farmers to pay higher wages or to automate? Why or why not?

• Do you think it is fair to demand that unemployed Canadian workers be forced to work on fruit farms at harvest time? If so, should unemployment insurance benefits be withheld from workers who refuse to work on fruit farms?

• Should people be forced to work in any area where they do not want to work?

• Should Canada draft any of the following people to work where laborers or special skills are required? Why or why not?
   —teachers in the far north
   —doctors in isolated areas

     –lawyers in slums
     –farm workers in rural areas at harvest time

• Some West Indian workers have come to depend on
the money they earn in Canada at harvest time.
     –If they still want to come and need the money, is it
     fair to refuse to hire those who have worked in Can-
     ada before?
     –Is it up to these imported workers to demand higher
     wages or better living conditions if they want them?

• Should these farm workers be allowed to stay in Canada after harvest season? Why or why not?

• Should East Indian workers brought to Canada to
work in the sawmill at Fort St. James also be sent home
after their work is done? Should Canadian citizens have
been found to fill their positions?

• Should an employer have a right to seek out workers
abroad who will accept the wage he is willing to offer
regardless of unemployment in Canada?

• Should the employer have the right to look anywhere
in Canada to find cheap labor?

• The native people have argued that imported labor
from abroad takes jobs that could go to unemployed
members of their people.
     –Should native people be given preference for employ-
     ment such as was available in Fort St. James?
     –Should the sawmill company be forced to employ
     native people? Why or why not?
     –Should native people be given preference over other
     unemployed Canadians?
     –Should either the government or the sawmill be re-
     sponsible for training native people so that they will
     be sufficiently skilled to take these jobs?

Analogy 2
Importing farm workers for a limited stay is not the only

way in which workers have been imported into Canada. Highly skilled and very well trained personnel have also been imported.

During the late 1950s and 1960s Canadian universities were expanding their facilities. New universities were being founded and older universities were increasing in size. To fill the sudden demand for qualified professors, Canadian universities looked outside Canada for personnel, especially in the United States.

More recently, the universities have slowed their growth. Enrollment has leveled off and demand for new university professors has decreased. As a result of the sudden expansion of Canadian universities, particularly of university graduate schools, an increasing number of qualified Canadians are now available for university teaching positions. Jobs, however, are scarce and some Canadians argue that Americans in teaching positions should now be replaced with Canadians or, at least, that no additional Americans should be hired.

• Do you believe that American professors should be removed from Canadian universities? Explain your answer.
   –Should American professors in Canadian universities be fired?
   –Should they be fired unless they become Canadian citizens?
   –Should they be kept on staff but refused promotions unless they become Canadian citizens?

• Do you believe that American professors should be ineligible to apply for new openings in Canadian universities?

• Should professors from England, France, or elsewhere be barred from positions at Canadian universities?

• Should Canadian universities hire the most qualified person to apply, no matter what that person's citizenship or place of birth is?

• Should a Canadian who is qualified but not the best

candidate to apply for a position be given preference over an American who seems to be the best candidate for the position? Why or why not?

• Would it be fair to hire American professors on condition that they would be replaced when equally qualified Canadians can be found?

• Would it be fair to replace the East Indians in Fort St. James when equally skilled native-born Canadians become available?

Community Life
• In the case of Fort St. James who of the following do you believe ought to have had responsibility in assisting the East Indians to integrate into the community?
  –the "Vancouver man" referred to by Ruth Hallock as "active in assisting East Indian people with job placement and immigration"
  –the mill owners who brought in East Indian "labourers as they were required"
  –the federal government which controls immigration
  –the provincial government which controls education and social services
  –the more established residents of Fort St. James
  –the East Indian immigrants

• In her letter, Ruth Hallock indicates that some of the East Indian customs or habits seemed either strange or objectionable to many other residents of Fort St. James. Is there anything the East Indians could have done or should have done to overcome community concerns?

• Would any of the following changes in East Indian habits or customs have been reasonable or unreasonable to demand? Which do you believe would be possible or impossible? Explain your answers.
  –East Indians should not live together in one area but should spread out around the town.
  –They should all learn English quickly.

–They should speak only English, even to one another.

–They should learn to eat foods without traditional spices.

–They should not haggle.

–They should not complain.

–They should only wear Western-style clothing.

–They should not walk together in groups.

• Is it fair to demand that immigrants change any of their traditional ways in order to be accepted into the Canadian community?

• In a democracy is it proper to demand that anyone change customs or habits because they seem odd or different to the majority? Explain your answers.

• Who in Fort St. James do you believe had the right to decide whether particular behavior, habits, or customs of East Indians must change?

–the government

–the employer

–the majority of town citizens

–the native people

–the East Indians

–only the individual

–none, all, or some of the above

Fighting and Racial Tension

• How does Ruth Hallock account for the street fighting between native people and East Indians? Do you agree with her analysis? Why or why not?

• An incident may set off a street fight but the reasons may be tangled in a long history of friction. How do you feel each of the following factors can affect the growth of friction?

–competition for jobs

–drinking

–racial hostility between groups

–the role of the established white community

–unequal numbers of male and female East Indian immigrants

• Can you suggest other factors which might have caused problems between native people and East Indians?

• After reading Ruth Hallock's letter, what steps do you believe could ensure that future fights do not take place?

• What role do you believe each of the following should take?

–the police
–the courts
–immigration authorities
–the government
–the schools
–the sawmill owners
–the older white community in Fort St. James
–the local native people
–the new East Indian Association
–the local newspaper

• Do you believe putting the brawlers in jail would serve a useful purpose when no serious injuries have been caused? Why or why not?

The Hallock Letter

• Ruth Hallock, who is the writer of this letter, is editor of the *Fort St. James Caledonia Courier*. Does the letter tell you more than you would expect to find in a newspaper story on this subject?

• Do Ruth Hallock's personal opinions come through in the letter? What do you think they are?

• From your reading of the letter what do you believe are her attitudes to each of the following?

–the fighting between East Indians and native people
–the role of the local police
–drinking
–the sawmill owners
–the social life of Fort St. James

• How do you think the opinions expressed in the letter would have been different if Ruth Hallock had been any of the following instead of local newspaper editor?

  –mayor of Fort St. James
  –an East Indian immigrant
  –the manager of the sawmill
  –a local school teacher
  –a liquor salesman
  –a member of the Necoslie Reserve
  –a tourist who saw the fight during a one-day visit to Fort St. James

• Do you believe, on the basis of your reading of this letter, that Ruth Hallock is attempting to be fair and objective?

5

St. Leonard

On the evening of Wednesday, 10 September 1969 the small Montreal suburb of St. Leonard was rocked by a major riot. At about 7:30 p.m. an estimated 1,500 demonstrators, ignoring a refusal by municipal authorities to grant them a parade permit, began a prearranged protest march into downtown St. Leonard. Local police, aided by police from surrounding municipalities and the Quebec Provincial Police, erected barricades to intercept the marchers en route. As demonstrators marched forward, helmeted police blocked their path. A clash was inevitable.

It is difficult, perhaps impossible, to isolate that single spark which ignited violence. There may have been many. At one point an angry group of about 500 marchers came headlong against a police barricade. Rather than stop, the marchers outflanked and surrounded the police. A Molotov cocktail was thrown. As flames lit the night sky, disciplined police retaliated with tear gas. Demonstrators broke ranks. Disorganized, they scattered into neighboring streets, setting additional fires and tripping fire and burglar alarms in a wave of store-window breaking. Protest placards were transformed into weapons against police billy-clubs. Violence and vandalism spread.

At exactly 9:04 p.m., St. Leonard's Mayor Leo Ouellet read the Riot Act. The blast of sirens was everywhere—from ambulances carrying away more than one hundred injured police and demonstrators; from fire trucks rushing from blaze to blaze; and from paddy wagons whisking demonstrators off to jail. Turmoil continued well into the night.

One Montreal newspaper reporter later recalled an incident at the Boulevard Shopping Centre near the spot where the march had begun a few hours earlier. In an ugly mood one group of protestors symbolically acted out their hostility.

> Someone in the crowd notices a Canadian flag, made up of hundreds of red and white light bulbs, and displayed on a wall about thirty feet above Greenberg's clothing store. For the next seven minutes they threw stones, sticks, and even railway spikes at the illuminated flag, smashing most of the bulbs.

The crowd cheered as each bulb shattered. Finally, darkness and a field of broken glass were all that remained of the flag.

The St. Leonard Riot, with its arrests, injuries, and thousands of dollars in property damage, did not erupt in a vacuum. Its origins led back to a dilemma which faced the parents of five- and six-year-old first graders in St. Leonard the year before the riot.

The suburb of St. Leonard had experienced rapid growth in the fifteen years before the riot. In the decade between 1956 and 1966 the population of this northern Montreal Island municipality had mushroomed from a mere 1,000 inhabitants to more than 25,000. Two years later, in 1968, the municipality of St. Leonard had grown by another 40 percent, to about 35,000 persons.

About 53 percent of the community's population in 1968 were French-Canadians. The remainder were largely foreign-born or the children of the foreign-born, especially Italians, Poles, and other Eastern Europeans. The Italian community, who made up nearly 27 percent of the population, represented the largest ethnic group in St. Leonard. The group commonly referred to as Anglo-Saxons in the community formed less than 2 percent of the St. Leonard population.

If the St. Leonard community was divided along ethnic lines, it was not divided on religious lines. The vast majority of St. Leonard's population, French-Canadians and non-French-Canadians alike, were Roman Catholics. This fact is especially important. In Quebec, there are two publicly supported educational systems separated on religious lines, one Protestant and one Roman Catholic. Thus, since nearly all residents of St. Leonard were Catholic, French-Canadian and non-French-Canadian children were all enrolled in the same elementary school system.

Until 1964, French was the only language of classroom instruction in St. Leonard. That year, bilingual instruction was introduced into several local schools after a number of New Canadian parents began to demand English-language classroom instruction for their children. The "bilingual system" was designed to offer a mixed French-English program with classroom instruction possible in either language. By 1968, the St. Leonard elementary school roll listed 3,500 children, mostly French-Canadians, receiving unilingual French-language instruction and another 1,300 children, largely from New Canadian families, receiving bilingual classroom instruction.

Organizing two different language streams within one school system proved an uneasy arrangement. On the one hand, parents of children in the bilingual stream, including many immigrants, recognized that fluency in

English offered their children a better chance in business, work, and higher education. They considered English the language of North American business. On the other hand, many French-Canadian parents, who were concerned for the survival of the French language in Quebec, sent their children to French-language elementary schools. They were angered that French-speaking Quebeckers would be at an economic disadvantage. In addition, many argued that immigrants to Quebec should be integrated into the French-Canadian community and, in their opinion, French-only schools were a necessary step in that direction.

Growing discontent finally surfaced in late autumn of 1967. On November 20, school commission member Leo Perusse introduced a resolution before the St. Leonard Roman Catholic School Commission which, if passed, would gradually phase out bilingual education in elementary schools of the municipality in favor of a French-only system. According to the resolution, those students already in the bilingual program would be allowed to complete their elementary education in bilingual classes. Perusse proposed, however, that beginning in September 1968, all grade one students entering St. Leonard schools be taught in French. The following year French-only classes would be extended to grade two and so on. Thus, by 1974, the bilingual stream in St. Leonard would be eliminated.

The resolution passed. A short study was undertaken to recommend practical methods for implementing the plan. The study, completed in only a few months, recognized that there could be resistance from those who wanted English in the schools and advised a one-year delay in implementing the resolution.

The threat that there would no longer be bilingual education in grade one, even if delayed one year, aroused the English-language supporters. In response to the study report a group of parents met and founded the English

Catholic Parents Association. On 11 March 1968, the new Association held a press conference. They demanded, as a minimum, that the English-French elementary school stream be retained and went on to propose English-only schools as another possibility. Just over a week later, more than 1,000 parents, including many recent Italian immigrants, crowded into the Jérôme le Royer school auditorium to hear the school commission officially agree to the proposed one-year delay in phasing out bilingual schools. However, the school commission firmly rejected any suggestion of an English-only school system. On March 25 the Association announced that it would field its own candidates in an upcoming election to fill two vacant seats on the St. Leonard Roman Catholic School Commission.

French-Canadian supporters of the original phase-out scheme feared that the one-year delay in implementing the plan would be repeated again year after year until the plan was killed forever. Following the example of English-language supporters, about forty French-language-supporter parents met and organized Le Mouvement Pour L'Intégration Scolaire (the Movement for School Integration), commonly referred to as the MIS. The MIS elected Raymond Lemieux as president and decided that they, too, would field candidates in the school commission election on a one-issue platform—all public schooling in St. Leonard must be in French.

Electioneering was heated and on 10 June 1968 the MIS won decisive victories in both seats. The results should not have surprised anyone since French-speaking residents of St. Leonard made up a small majority of the population. In addition, many supporters of the English Catholic Parents Association's pro-English candidates were immigrants who had not been in Canada long enough to gain Canadian citizenship. As a result, they could not vote.

The newly elected MIS members, together with a MIS

supporter already on the school commission, took control of the five-man board. In a quick move the new commission succeeded in rescinding the earlier one-year delay in phasing out bilingual elementary education. Beginning in September 1968 all grade one students entering St. Leonard schools were to be placed in French-only classrooms.

The MIS election victory and subsequent reversal of the one-year delay in the phase-out plan generated increased tension within St. Leonard. This tension was further aggravated in a related school protest demonstration.

Although elementary schools of St. Leonard are the responsibility of the local school commission, high schools fall under the separate jurisdiction of the Le Royer Regional School Board, which covers several adjoining municipalities of which St. Leonard is one. The Le Royer Board designated the Aimé-Renaud high school, situated in St. Leonard, to become an English-language high school beginning in September 1968. French-speaking students attending the school were to move to French-language high schools operated elsewhere by the Le Royer Board. While this student shuffle was merely an administrative move which had nothing to do with the St. Leonard School Commission's plan to phase out English classes in elementary schools, the two separate events became entangled in the heat of the moment.

Just before midnight on Friday, 30 August 1968, a group of French-speaking students occupied the Aimé-Renaud high school with the support of the MIS. Aided by their parents and French-speaking teachers who picketed outside, the student protesters set up barricades at the school doors and phoned a French-language radio station in Montreal to report their demand that Aimé-Renaud not be made an English-language high school. Students with walkie-talkies patrolled their captured territory and bedding and food were slipped in through windows. The protest was well organized and the building was kept clean.

The occupation lasted a full week. Eventually there were more than 100 students inside the school and more supporters parading outside with placards, including one sign which read "Unilingual Yes—Bilingual No."

Intervention by the Quebec Minister of Education, Jean-Guy Cardinal, became necessary before the occupation ended. The result was a victory for the protesters. Aimé-Renaud would open for the school year as a French-language high school. English-speaking students would be enrolled in other schools.

While the Aimé-Renaud occupation was going on, the English Catholic Parents Association took drastic action to regain bilingual elementary school classes. They called for a boycott of the St. Leonard elementary schools. The Association and its president, Robert Beale, organized a boycott to keep all children of their supporters out of public schools until bilingual education was once again guaranteed in St. Leonard. The boycott was effective. An estimated 84 percent of those students enrolled in the bilingual stream stayed home. Only forty-three non-French-Canadian children eligible for grade one enrolled. Almost nine times as many stayed home.

As the boycott dragged on, however, parents became increasingly concerned that their children were being deprived of an education. They sought to find another method to pressure for bilingual schools. As a countermove, the Association sent all children back to school on October 2, except those who would be entering grade one, now available only in French. Privately funded bilingual classes were quickly organized for the grade one pupils.

Six bilingual classes of thirty students each were established. When twenty-five more students than were expected registered, they were not turned away. Six instructors were hired, two retired teachers from Montreal, three teachers who had previously left the school system to raise families, and one recent teachers' college graduate. A special French-language teacher was eventually hired to work with each class on a rotating basis.

In makeshift classrooms in converted basement recreation rooms or other space volunteered to the Association, classes quickly got under way. The official Quebec grade one curriculum was followed as closely as possible.

The price tag for these boycott classes was high. Even with many facilities and supplies donated by supporters and tuition paid by those parents who could afford it, the Association found it difficult to raise the necessary $5,000 to $6,000 a month to meet salary and school bills. As the school year advanced, the Association's debts grew. Hoped-for financial assistance from the government of Quebec was denied in January 1969.

As winter gave way to spring it became increasingly clear to the Association that so long as the boycott classes continued, financial problems would worsen. By June, the first year's boycott ended with a deficit estimated between $20,000 and $30,000. The prospect for the following year was bleak indeed. After all, the following year the Association would be faced with operating not only grade one classes but classes for grade two students as well.

Efforts to resolve the St. Leonard school issue finally reached the offices of the Quebec Minister of Education. On May 21, Cardinal met with a delegation of pro-English supporters. During the meeting Cardinal reportedly agreed that the provincial government would assume the Association's debt and assist in the organization of a private school in St. Leonard for children who wished English-language education. Existing legislation, he pointed out on television three months later, allowed the government of Quebec to pay 80 percent of the cost of recognized private schools.

76

Lemieux and the MIS took only two days to reject any suggestion of English-language private schools to be set up in St. Leonard. A meeting to protest the private school plan was organized by the MIS for Wednesday, 3 September, only four days before schools were scheduled to open for the 1969 school year. The meeting turned into a battle. In the packed hall pro-English-language Association supporters heckled Lemieux and other MIS speakers. Shouting matches in French, English, and Italian turned into fist fights. Chairs were thrown and the fighting between the two groups spread to the street where it took police three hours to establish order.

The following day supporters of bilingual education also rejected any private school plan. They also would not compromise—they demanded the right to English-language instruction in public schools which they supported with their tax dollars. They argued that English-language schooling was their right and they wanted it in public not private schools.

As was the case a year earlier, when school opened most non-French-speaking students stayed home. Once again boycott classes were organized, this time for grades one and two, and renting an unoccupied apartment building as a school was proposed. Tempers approached the boiling point.

The MIS called for a protest march for Wednesday, September 10, to reaffirm its determination to continue with the phase out of bilingual education in the schools. St. Leonard police, fearing violence, denied the marchers a parade permit. The marchers went ahead with their parade plans and, as already described, the result was a riot.

Following the riot, the neighboring Montreal Protestant School Board offered to find room in its system for St. Leonard school children wanting English-language instruction. The offer was accepted by parents. Catholic students in St. Leonard who wanted classroom instruction in English were bussed to Protestant schools in Montreal. Everyone recognized that this situation was a temporary solution at best.

Postscript

Since the St. Leonard episode, the Government of Quebec has found it difficult to establish a fixed policy on the issue of language rights in general, and language of classroom instruction in particular. Any action, one way or the other, generated hostility from one group of language supporters or the other.

In the wake of the St. Leonard uproar the Government of Quebec passed legislation (Bill 63) which ensured parents the freedom of choice in selecting the language of instruction for their children. The practical effect of this legislation was that immigrants and children of immigrants continued to move into the English-language stream in schools.

Advocates of French-language instruction in the classroom continually attacked this law. They charged that this bill perpetuated second-class status for the French language in Quebec. The legislation, they argued, created better economic opportunities for immigrants who chose the English-language stream since employers would prefer English-speaking or bilingual employees until French was made mandatory.

On 21 May 1974 the Bourassa government reacted to this criticism. It announced plans for a new bill to replace Bill 63. The new Bill 22 imposes conditions on parents' freedom of choice, especially for immigrants and children of immigrants. According to the bill, only children who already had an adequate knowledge of English would be admitted to English-language schools. Any immigrant child who came to Quebec speaking neither English nor French would be enrolled in a French-language school. Parents lose freedom of choice, but French-language survival in Quebec would be one step closer.

Children who apply for entry into English-language schools would be required to take an English-language proficiency test. There is fear that children born in Quebec but raised in homes where the language of conversation is neither French nor English would find it difficult to pass such a test. Accordingly, these children would be forced into French-language schools against the will of their parents.

Immigrant communities in Quebec responded to the proposed Bill 22 with immediate hostility. While most immigrant parents seem to recognize the benefits to their children of knowing both French and English, they are angered over any attempt to limit English-language instruction. The publisher of a Montreal Italian newspaper protested, "The right to choose our language in the schools must not be taken away." A spokesman for a Montreal Greek community committee studying the proposed bill warned, "We are going to fight the legislation. It is unfair. We want our children to be able to compete in the world of today and it demands that they know both languages."

Protest failed. Before school opened in September 1974, Bill 22 had become law.

The Issues

• Should English-language classroom instruction continue with government support in St. Leonard?

Language in the Schools
• Canada is officially a bilingual country. Should children in all Canadian schools learn English and French as a matter of routine? Why or why not?

Analogy 1
The parents of St. Leonard who want their children to

study in English as part of a bilingual education are not alone in arguing the importance of language instruction in the schools. Elsewhere in Canada the language issue has also generated controversy and parent demands, but with an important difference. Outside of Quebec, provinces have not offered as comprehensive a publicly supported school system in both English and French. Most parents outside Quebec who want their children to attend French-language schools or bilingual schools similar to those which exist in St. Leonard must either seek out private schools at their own expense or be lucky enough to live in one of the few areas where publicly supported schools working in the French language are operating.

• Do you agree that Quebec should support schools in two different languages while the other provinces do not?

• Is it fair to demand that provinces with little or no demand for schools which teach in a second language be forced to set up schools in the other official language?

• Is it their duty to do so if Canada is to be bilingual?

• If Canada is to be truly bilingual, is it just as important for those who now speak French to be forced to learn and study in English as it is for English-speaking students to do so in French? Why or why not?

• What do you think are the advantages in knowing how to speak both English and French? Would there be any disadvantages for you?

• Many French-Canadians feel that if English and French have equal status in Quebec it would not have the same degree of impact as elsewhere in Canada. They feel that since French language usage has gradually decreased in Canada as a whole, as well as in North America as a whole, special care must be taken to ensure the primacy of French in Quebec. Equality of English and French in Quebec would, they fear, only lead to the eventual elimination of French.

80

–Do you agree? Why or why not?

–Are these fears enough of a reason not to have bilingualism?

• Should everyone in Canada be encouraged to read, write, and speak both English and French?

–Should it be a condition of promotion in the federal public service?

–Should it be a condition in university enrollment? business promotion? gaining Canadian citizenship?

• Should bilingualism be compulsory?

Analogy 2

While Canada is officially a bilingual country with English and French as the two recognized languages, they are not the only languages spoken by Canadians. Immigrants from all over the world have come to Canada and many would like to retain and encourage use of their languages within their groups. The native people of Canada also have their own languages and have become increasingly interested in having these languages flourish. For the most part, schools have been interested only in ensuring that each student learn English or French. They have generally opposed classroom instruction in languages other than English (or French in Quebec) although some schools do offer study of immigrant languages as a subject—never as a language of instruction. Some native Canadian and New Canadian parents claim, on the other hand, that as citizens and taxpayers they also want their own language given a place in the schools. Few, if any, would argue that English or French should not be learned, but some feel that if their children should be bilingual it should be in the majority language of their area and the language of the home, whether that be Ukrainian, Chinese, Cree, or Italian.

• Is there a difference between teaching a language as a subject and using that language for classroom instruction? If so, what is the difference?

• What is the point of teaching students to use another language in the schools, any language, if they will never get an opportunity to use that language?

• Should languages other than English or French be taught in the schools?

• Should languages other than English or French be used as the language of classroom instruction in the schools?

• If a large group of native people or immigrants from a particular country are located in a school district do you believe that their language should be taught in the local elementary school? High school? Why or why not?

• In the case where a large number of children speaking a language other than English or French enter a school, do you believe that regular classroom instruction in that other language for subjects such as history and mathematics should be allowed?

• Should there be some rule about language use to apply to all schools in Canada? Should each case be judged on its own merits? How would you evaluate the request for non-English-language classroom instruction in each of the following cases? Explain your answer.

–A group of French-Canadians wish a publicly supported French-language school in Prince Edward Island.

–A group of immigrants to Canada from France want a French-language school in Prince Edward Island.

–A group of Italian immigrants to Canada want a French-language school in Prince Edward Island.

–A group of Italian immigrants to Canada want Italian to be taught as a subject in their local school.

–A group of Italian immigrants to Canada want Italian to be used as the language of classroom instruction until their children know English (or French).

–A group of Italian immigrants to Canada want some subjects in the school to be taught in Italian so their children will be encouraged to retain their Italian-language skills.

–A group of Cree Indians living in a city want their language to be used as a language of instruction in their local school.

–A group of Cree Indians on the reserve wish their language to be used as the language of instruction in the reserve school.

• Would you object if any of the preceding cases were accomplished in private schools and not at public expense?

• What arguments could you make for or against each of the following positions?

–If Canada is going to be strong and united, we should all speak one language and that language should be English.

–If Canada is going to be strong and united, we should all speak English and French equally well.

–If Canada is going to be strong and united, we should all speak one language and that language should be English, except in Quebec where there should be a free choice between English and French.

• If the culture of Quebec is to be respected, should everyone in Quebec speak both English and French?

• If the culture of Quebec is to be respected, should everyone in Quebec speak only French?

• If Canada is going to be strong and united should it be nobody's business what languages are spoken in the home or in private so long as people can get by in English or French as is necessary for their work and safety?

St. Leonard

• Who do you believe should have had the right to decide whether English should be used as a language of classroom instruction in St. Leonard schools?

–the local school board

–those parents who want English-language instruction

–the majority of all parents in St. Leonard whether they are for or against

–the provincial government

–the federal government

–the students

• Once a democratic election had decided school board membership and the school board had decided to phase out English-language instruction, should all parents have gone along with the decision? Why or why not?

• Do you believe the boycott was justified?

• If you lived in St. Leonard and wanted English-language instruction for your child entering grade one, what would you have done? Are any of the following reasonable alternatives? Explain.

–Join the boycott and send the child to the special schools organized by the Association.

–Give your child what English-language teaching was possible at home but otherwise send the child to the now French-language-only public schools.

–Give up your job, sell your house, and move into Montreal where English-language instruction is still available.

–Give up your job, sell your house, and move to Victoria where you can be sure English-language instruction will always be available.

• Do you believe Bill 22 is just? If not, what alternative would you suggest?

The Riot

• Who do you believe was responsible for the St. Leonard riot on the evening of 10 September 1969?

–the MIS and its supporters

–opponents of the MIS

–the police
–St. Leonard municipal authorities
–all of the above
–none of the above

• Should the MIS request for a parade permit have been granted?

• Should the MIS have canceled its demonstration for 10 September since there had been violence between MIS supporters and their opponents the night before?

• What would you have done if you were St. Leonard's Mayor Leo Ouellet and felt that a parade by the MIS might spark a confrontation with the anti-MIS group?
  –Reject the parade permit and use police disperse markers.
  –Allow the parade and try to use police to protect marchers from opposition or to guard against marchers turning the parade into a violent protest on their own.
  –Allow the protest march as long as it were rerouted away from the centers of non-MIS support.
  –Let the march go on as planned and keep police away so the MIS and anti-MIS groups could do as they pleased.

• Do you believe a solution, even a temporary solution, to the St. Leonard school issue could have been worked out before the riot?

• Immediately following the riot, a Montreal Protestant School Board offer to temporarily absorb those St. Leonard children who wanted English-language instruction was accepted. What do you think would have been the response of the following groups if the offer had been made before the riot? Explain your answer.
  –pro-English-language parents
  –pro-French-language parents
  –the St. Leonard Roman Catholic School Commission
  –the government of Quebec

6

The Ontario Science Centre Demonstration

On 17 October 1971, one of the most powerful political figures in the world arrived in Ottawa. With military honor guard, government and diplomatic officials on hand, Soviet Premier Alexei Kosygin began a nine-day visit to Canada at the invitation of the Canadian government.

The Kosygin visit, which followed an earlier trip by Prime Minister Trudeau to the Soviet Union, symbolized the opening of a new and, hopefully, friendlier era in Soviet–Canadian relations. After many years of distrust the cold war between East and West seemed to be thawing. For both Canada and the Soviet Union greater trade, travel, and scientific cooperation now appeared possible. The Kosygin visit, the Canadian public was advised, would help to cement these better relations.

The schedule for Kosygin's visit had been laid out well in advance of his arrival. It included a mixture of formal meetings with Canadian officials in Ottawa on matters of mutual concern and a somewhat less formal series of visits to other Canadian cities where special events had been arranged. According to plan, Kosygin and his party, which included his daughter Lyudmilla Gvishiani, would stop in Ottawa, Montreal, Vancouver, Edmonton, and, for their last stop, Toronto. Once in Toronto Kosygin was to make side trips to inspect the General Motors plant in Oshawa and Ontario Hydro's nuclear power station at Pickering, just east of Toronto. For the evening of 25 October a banquet in Kosygin's honor was to be given by the Canadian Manufacturers' Association in the Great Hall of the Ontario Science Centre in northeastern Toronto.

Even with the much publicized improvement in Canadian–Soviet relations, security for the Kosygin party was tight, perhaps tighter than it had ever been for any other official visitors in Canadian history, including the Royal Family. The Premier was said to have brought his own personal security guards with him, members of the Soviet secret police; under international law it is the ultimate responsibility of Canadian officials to protect visitors to Canada. Accordingly, Canadian police organized their own protective blanket around the Premier and his party.

A special task force of the Royal Canadian Mounted Police was organized especially to coordinate Kosygin's security. The task was complex. Not only did it involve the cooperation of Soviet security authorities, but it also required the full support of provincial and municipal police forces at every stop along the Kosygin route.

Government and police officials felt that there was good reason for extraordinary security measures. In spite of improving Canadian–Soviet relations, few Canadians were sympathetic to Communism. Indeed, some groups in Canada appeared openly hostile to specific Soviet policies including the treatment of religious and ethnic groups in the Soviet Union, matters which the Soviet government insists are nobody's business but its own.

Among the thousands of men and women who came to Canada after the Hungarian revolt in 1956 and the

Czechoslovakian uprising in 1967 are many who still harbor bitter memories of the Soviet role in crushing their rebellions. In addition, organizers of security for the Kosygin visit were well aware that various other groups of Canadians were upset by what was seen as Soviet policies designed to suppress groups within the Soviet Union itself. Canadian Jews, for instance, had become increasingly concerned for the welfare of Jews in the Soviet Union, who they claimed were being systematically denied basic human rights. Furthermore, the best avenue of escape was closed: they were generally refused permission to emigrate from the Soviet Union. The Canadian Jewish community, through the Canadian Jewish Congress, announced plans to publicize its concern and, hopefully, to influence a change in Soviet policy through a series of peaceful protest demonstrations wherever Kosygin and his party went in Canada.

In similar moves, Canadians of Baltic descent (from Estonia, Latvia, and Lithuania) and Ukrainians made plans for their own anti-Soviet demonstrations. Those of Baltic extraction were enraged at the Soviet Union's absorption of their once independent homelands into the Soviet Union early in the Second World War. Even though more than thirty years had passed since the Soviet move, members of the relatively small Canadian Baltic community hoped to use the Kosygin visit as an opportunity to make their demand for freedom and independence of the Baltic states known to the public in general and Kosygin in particular.

The Canadian Ukrainian community is many times larger than the Baltic group. It has also been in Canada much longer. There has been hardly any Ukrainian immigration to Canada in the past twenty years. In fact, much of the present Ukrainian community in Canada can trace its roots back to the large agricultural immigration which came into Canada from Eastern Europe between 1896 and 1914. The Ukrainian community is thus into its third or fourth generation in Canada. Many Ukrainian Canadians, however, have never lost their sense of community, nor their deep attachment for Ukrainian culture and the Ukraine itself, now a state within the Soviet Union.

In recent years a large part of the Canadian Ukrainian community had become angered by what it termed the "Russification of the Ukraine" by the Soviet government. The language and culture of the Ukraine, it was argued during the Kosygin visit, was being systematically and ruthlessly suppressed by the Soviet authorities in favor of Russian language and culture. Ukrainian Canadians claimed that the Soviet government was trying to undermine any lingering hopes that the Ukraine would or could ever become an independent nation among nations.

To many Canadians of Ukrainian descent, the Kosygin visit offered them an opportunity to demonstrate their hostility to this alleged "Russification" policy. Under the auspices of the Ukrainian Canadian Committee a series of peaceful protests were planned.

Beginning with his visit to Ottawa and throughout the first week in Canada, Kosygin met anti-Soviet demonstrations all along his route. The generally peaceful protesters received wide press, radio, and television coverage, not just in Canada but also well beyond Canada's borders. The Kosygin trip to Canada was world news with coverage by the *New York Times, The Times* of London, and American TV networks, to name only a few. To the protesters, therefore, it did not seem to matter that Kosygin and his party tended to ignore them. The demonstrators' audience had grown worldwide and, it was hoped, the Soviet government would eventually feel pressure from world public opinion.

While police believed that they would be able to cope with peaceful demonstrators, an incident took place in Ottawa which caused security officials to fear that not all demonstrators would indeed be peaceful. As Prime

Minister Trudeau and Soviet Premier Kosygin walked from the main entrance of the Parliament Buildings to a waiting car, Geza Matrai, a Hungarian refugee and anti-Communist activist, broke through police lines. Before security guards could catch him, Matrai tackled the Soviet Premier. Matrai was quickly subdued and arrested. The Premier was unharmed. However, the assault itself, seen on television around the world, underlined the need for tight security and the risks of any hole in security arrangements.

The potential conflict between demands for maximum security of Kosygin and the right of Canadians to demonstrate their opposition to Soviet policy came to a head in front of the Ontario Science Centre in Toronto. A banquet in honor of Premier Kosygin was arranged for the evening of Monday, 25 October, in the Great Hall of the Science Centre, near the hotel where Kosygin and his party were staying. Kosygin had earlier expressed a desire to meet with Canadian industrial and business leaders, so, in the planning for the Kosygin visit, Prime Minister Trudeau asked the Canadian Manufacturers' Association to host the Science Centre dinner, which it agreed to do.

Demonstrators planned their own reception for Kosygin. With the cooperation of Toronto police officials, the Canadian Jewish Congress planned for about 10,000 members of the Jewish community to take part in a protest march and vigil the night of the banquet. It was decided that the Jewish demonstrators would gather in a park across from the hotel where Kosygin and his party were staying and march about half a mile to a large vacant lot across from the northeast corner of the fifty-five-acre Ontario Science Centre grounds.

On the evening of Monday, 25 October an estimated 12,000 persons, somewhat more than had been expected, assembled. Carrying signs, some of which bore the slogan "Let My People Go," the Jewish protest group marched to the vacant lot where they listened to an address by author Elie Wiesel on the difficult problems of Jews in the Soviet Union. Within an hour the demonstrators dispersed as peacefully as they had gathered.

The protest demonstration planned by the Ukrainian Canadian Committee took a far different turn. Like the Jewish community, the Ukrainian Canadian Committee wished to assemble near the Ontario Science Centre to show their hostility to Soviet policy. A subcommittee was organized to plan the protest. The subcommittee, chaired by Robert Ihor Maksymec, knew that the Ukrainian protest would have to conform with police security arrangements for the Kosygin dinner They met with police and seemingly reached an agreement that their group would meet in an open area across the street from the southern tip of the Ontario Science Centre grounds. Assuming that the exact location of the demonstration had been settled, the subcommittee went off to continue with its preparations.

Ukrainian-language radio programs announced the forthcoming demonstration, congregations at Ukrainian Catholic churches were asked to attend, and pamphlets in English and Ukrainian were distributed requesting people to come.

Calling for an "orderly and dignified" demonstration, the pamphlets also pinpointed the open space to the south of the Science Centre as the gathering point for the Ukrainian meeting; organized picketing in front of the Science Centre was also promised. As the pamphlets explained in Ukrainian:

> We are calling upon the Ukrainians in Toronto and Western Ontario to take part in an orderly well organized demonstration against Premier of U.S.S.R., Alexei Kosygin, representative of Russian-Bolshevik Imperialism and Tyranny.

Unknown to the small committee planning the protest,

92

a hitch developed. While arranging exact security for the Kosygin banquet, police decided that the street which marks the Science Centre's southern boundary must be reserved as an alternate route for Kosygin's exit from the Science Centre should any difficulty with the first route arise. As a result, no demonstrators were to be allowed near this road. The Ukrainian community, which still planned to assemble along the south side of that very road, was not informed of the new police arrangements. Police did not designate any other location for the Ukrainian protest.

Kosygin and his party arrived at the Ontario Science Centre without incident early in the evening.

When Maksymec and other officials of the Ukrainian organizing subcommittee arrived on the scene they were informed by police officials that the protest group could not meet to the south of the Science Centre as they had expected. The police could offer the Ukrainians no alternative spot to meet. As police officials later explained, they were not in the business of setting up places for protest demonstrations.

The Ukrainian demonstrators, joined by many other anti-Soviet protesters, began to arrive. It had been raining on and off during the day, so many carried umbrellas. Ukrainian organizers tried to maintain some discipline, but their plans were ruined for lack of a meeting place. An estimated 4,000 to 5,000 persons slowly collected at random on the sidewalks, front yards, and intersections across from the front of the Ontario Science Centre.

In spite of the poor location and the unsettled weather, the crowd was good natured. So were the police officers on the spot. People joked and sang. Police seemed relaxed. More than 700 police were on duty in the Science Centre area, about 300 of these assigned directly to crowd control in front of the Science Centre. In addition to a horse-mounted unit, an Emergency Task Force trained in riot control, paddy wagons, riot control equipment, and ambulances were on hand. It was hoped that they would not be needed.

Just after seven o'clock, witnesses later recalled, the mood began to change. According to an official report on the demonstration, the crowd at one point seemed to sway forward into the street as if pushed from behind. It may never be known what caused the crowd to move forward a few feet, but the police were thus forced into a holding action. As camera bulbs flashed and network television lights lit up the area, police locked arms to push the crowd back. Caught between the wall of police in front and a pushing crowd behind, people in the middle began to panic. Some fell. A scuffle broke out. Police lifted one person bodily over the heads of the crowd and into the street to a nearby paddy wagon.

Upset by the arrest, some members of the crowd threw lighted candles they carried as symbols of their protest. Several police were struck. Shouts and excited remarks such as "The Science Centre is for the public!" were heard as the disturbance spread.

The crowd grew more unruly and the police mounted unit was called into action. Ten police on horseback, most with riding crops in hand, rode into the crowd near the spot where the demonstrators had first swayed forward. With only a limited area of open space behind them into which to retreat, it was difficult for the tightly packed crowd to get out of the way of the horses. Some people fell and were trampled. Police on foot following the mounted unit arrested anyone who blocked their path.

According to the official report on the incident, an elderly woman who attended the demonstration with her husband fell as she sought to avoid a horse. Lying on the ground she was struck by the horse's hooves as it passed over her. Luckily, she was barely harmed, although she did suffer shock. Meanwhile her husband was hit several times by a riding crop as he went to the defense of his wife with an umbrella. He, too, suffered shock.

In another case, a man was struck on the head with a riding crop as he tried to help a teen-age girl who had fallen during the first move by horses into the crowd. The man required eleven stitches. Several police officers received minor injuries.

In all, eighteen people were arrested. They included high-school and university students, the manager of a fuel-oil firm, a mortgage broker, and a businessman from London, Ontario, who had come to the demonstration with his son and two daughters.

The outbreak lasted only a few minutes. When it was over, what had set out to be a peaceful demonstration was a shambles. Most of the crowd dispersed, leaving only a few people standing in front of the Ontario Science Centre when Soviet Premier Kosygin left the banquet at 9:30 P.M., unaware of the incident that had taken place. The next morning he flew to Cuba.

The Issues

• Who was responsible for the outbreak of violence in front of the Ontario Science Centre on the evening of 25 October 1971?

Canadians and Internal Soviet Policy
• Should the Canadian government in any way become involved in whether or not the Ukraine keeps its language and culture alive?

• Should the Canadian government in any way become involved in whether or not the Soviet Union lets its Jewish population migrate if they want to do so?

• Do you feel it is proper for Canadian citizens to request that their government interfere in the internal affairs of another country? Should the Canadian government use its influence to pressure for change in domestic policy of a foreign government?

• Who is to decide what is an internal or domestic policy? The Soviet Union claims that the question of Ukrainian or Jewish interests in that country are internal Soviet affairs. Do you agree?

• Which of the following cases are internal affairs of the country concerned and therefore no business of anyone else or any other country? Which do you believe are not solely internal affairs? Why?

(a) In 1968 the Nigerian state of Biafra declared its independence from Nigeria. Nigeria refused to recognize the independence of Biafra. During the bloody civil war which followed, the independence of Biafra was crushed. Nigeria claimed that this was an internal affair of no concern to anyone else.

(b) During 1972 the Government of Uganda confiscated the property and ordered the expulsion of thousands of East Asians living in Uganda but not citizens of Uganda. The East Asians left. Many of them came to Canada. Uganda claimed that this was an internal affair.

(c) The government of South Africa has long been practicing a policy of racial separation called apartheid. This policy has led to the almost complete subjugation and control of the majority black population in South Africa by the minority white population. South Africa claims that this is an internal affair.

(d) Japan and the Soviet Union have developed fishing vessels which virtually sweep the sea clean of fish, and are using them in international waters. If these ships continue to operate freely in international waters, Canadian fishermen fear that fish stocks may be threatened in the near future. Both Japan and the Soviet Union claim that so long as their ships remain in international waters, they are not subject to interference from any country.

(e) In 1972 the United States set off an underground atomic explosion on Amchitka Island, Alaska, and in 1974 India exploded its first atomic device. Both the United States and India claimed that these were internal affairs.

(f) In 1973 a group of American Indians took over the small town of Wounded Knee, South Dakota, in protest against a long history of mistreatment of native people. State and federal police surrounded Wounded Knee until the Indians surrendered and were arrested. American authorities claimed that this was an internal affair.

• What cases can you suggest in which a country has argued that its actions are an internal affair, but that you feel are matters of international concern?

• In the United States, a Soviet–American trade treaty, which would open the door to increased business between the two world powers, was stalled in the American Senate. The Senate, which must ratify treaties before they are official, delayed ratification because of the Soviet refusal to allow its religious and ethnic minorities, especially Jews, freedom to migrate. The Soviet Union, which wants the trade treaty, is reportedly looking for ways to meet the Senate's condition without too much publicity.

–Do you believe the Senate's action was proper?

–Is it a form of blackmail or just good bargaining?

–Would it be justified if the Soviet Union now allows its minorities to migrate? Would it be justified if the Soviet Union did not let its minorities migrate?

–Should it be any concern of the Senate what the Soviet Union does with its minorities?

• Agricultural workers in California and the American southwest have been on strike against local fruit growers, especially grape and lettuce growers. While growers argue that this is simply a local labor/management question, the strikers have asked Canadians, who make up a big market for California products, to boycott California grapes and lettuce. The strikers claim that such a boycott would help them win the strike.

  –Should it matter to Canadians who wins this strike?
  –Do you believe working conditions of grape pickers in the United States is any business of Canadians? Why or why not?
  –Is a boycott justified?
  –Do you believe the strikers are using the boycott as a form of blackmail or as good bargaining?

• Can any country ever claim that all domestic policies and actions are not the concern of anyone else?

Parallel Situation
In 1967 Canada celebrated its centennial year. One of the highlights of the one hundredth anniversary of Confederation was the Expo '67 World's Fair in Montreal which attracted millions of visitors from around the world.

Among the most important world figures to visit Montreal during the centennial was Charles de Gaulle, President of France. Most visits to Canada by foreign government leaders were seen by the Canadian government and people as a friendly gesture and a salute to Canada during its centennial. But de Gaulle's visit was long regretted by many Canadians.

Instead of going first to Ottawa, Canada's capital, as was expected of such important foreign visitors, de Gaulle stayed in the province of Quebec. This break with formality would probably have been ignored had de Gaulle not violated what the Canadian government regarded as a more important rule for visiting foreign government leaders. He interfered in Canada's internal affairs. In a speech delivered to a crowd in front of Montreal city hall, de Gaulle outlined the historical roots of France's connection with French Canada and expressed sympathy with French-Canadian "national" aspirations.

98

He concluded his remarks with the now famous remark, "Vive le Québec libre!"—Long live free Quebec!—the slogan of the Quebec separatists.

The Canadian government responded immediately. Prime Minister Lester Pearson claimed that de Gaulle was voicing support for separatist elements in Quebec. In a sharply worded reply the Prime Minister protested against de Gaulle's meddling in Canada's internal affairs "as unacceptable," that problems which might exist with regard to Quebec were no concern of the president of France. De Gaulle left Canada the next day.

• Do you believe de Gaulle was meddling in Canadian affairs?

• Do you think de Gaulle had a right to make the statement?

• Would it still be meddling:
  –if de Gaulle had said "Vive le Québec libre!" in France instead of in Canada?
  –if he had said it to a pro-Quebec separatist rally in France?
  –if he had said it privately to Prime Minister Pearson during a visit by Pearson to France?
  –if it had been shouted at Pearson by pro-separatist supporters during a visit by Pearson to France?

• How is the Canadian government's relationship with Quebec and French-Canadians the same or different from the Soviet Union's relationship with Ukrainians and Jews in the Soviet Union?

• Is the issue of Quebec in Canada solely a matter of Canadian internal affairs? Why?

• Can any issue ever truly be internal to one country and thus be no one else's business?

The Demonstration
• Do you believe that Canadians of Urkainian, Baltic, or

Jewish extraction had a right to demonstrate against Kosygin?

• Is it appropriate for citizens of Canada to demonstrate against foreign political leaders who are guests of the Canadian government? Why or why not?

• In planning for their protest, was it the responsibility of the Ukrainian Canadian Committee to check back with the police to ensure that the original demonstration site was still available?

• Should the police have informed the Ukrainian Canadian Committee of the change in plans which took away the Committee's demonstration site?

• When demonstration organizers arrived at the Science Centre to find their site was no longer available, should they have called off their protest? Could they have called off their protest even if they had wanted to do so? What would you have done?

• Do you believe police should have helped the Committee find a new location for their demonstration? Should they have done so even at the last minute?

• The police later claimed they were not in the business of finding places for people to demonstrate. Whose responsibility is it? Do you believe it is the duty of the police to assist demonstrators to find a protest site? Was it their duty in this case? What do you believe the duties of police should be toward demonstrators at a protest?

• Once the crowd had gathered in a disorganized fashion across from the Science Centre, do you think demonstration organizers should or could have tried to carry out their original program of prayer, speeches, and song?

• Once the crowd had gathered, what could the police have done?
– forcefully dispersed the crowd at once
– hold the crowd back in a limited space
– clear the street so demonstrators could have an instant

demonstration site

• Can you think of any other options?

• Do you feel that horses should be used for crowd control? Why or why not? In your opinion, without use of horses at the Science Centre would the violence have grown worse? Would it have been less?

• What part did press and television coverage play at the protest? Do you believe there would have been any protest at all if press and television had been absent? Should they have been excluded? Explain your position.

• In what ways do you feel that the violence might have been prevented? Could it have been prevented? In what ways could the violence have been lessened?

7

The Green Paper Debate

As much as any other country in the world, Canada is a land of immigrants. Millions of Canadian citizens were born in other countries and still more millions are the children or grandchildren of immigrants to Canada. Indeed, some argue that immigration has been as important to the growth of Canadian population, economy, and cultural identity as has been natural increase through children born in Canada. In 1974/75 Canada's population grew more as a result of immigration from abroad than it did from natural increase through childbirth. Not only has Canada welcomed immigration, but it has also actively encouraged immigration with advertising and with resettlement programs.

In recent years government and public had begun to reconsider immigration policy. Questions have been raised about the economic and social role of the immigrant in Canada. As Canadians become population conscious, especially with respect to the mushrooming size of urban areas and problems of population size, pollution, unemployment, and energy consumption, the place of immigration in Canadian development becomes a major issue.

In September 1973 the Minister of Manpower and Immigration, Robert Andras, informed the Commons that a comprehensive review of Canadian immigration policy was to be undertaken. The review would, the Minister indicated, become the basis for a new Immigration Act which, he hoped, could be introduced shortly after the study was completed. A small task force of officials, researchers, and immigration experts were gathered together in Ottawa under the chairmanship of Richard M. Tait, loaned for this review from the Department of External Affairs. The task force was named the Canadian Immigration and Population Study.

The task was not easy. The group studied briefs and letters from community, national, ethnic, and other organizations and interested members of the public, held discussions with other government agencies in federal and provincial jurisdictions, and commissioned eight supplementary reports on various immigration related topics from outside consultants. All of this was reviewed, analyzed, and weighed in consideration of the task force's report.

After spending more than a year and $500,000 in deliberations, the Task Force completed its work. On 3 February 1975 the Report of the Canadian Immigration and Population Study was tabled in the House of Commons. The Report, in four volumes, is collectively called the Green Paper on Immigration Policy. Each volume approaches the issues of immigration from a different perspective. The first volume, entitled *Immigration Policy Perspectives*, considers possible alternatives in immigration policy, the reasons for and possible results of each alternative. The second volume, *The Immigration Program*, outlines the workings of past and present immigration policies and procedures. Statistics on Canadian immigration and population growth make up the third volume, appropriately titled *Immigration and Popu-*

lation Statistics. Lastly, a volume entitled *Three Years in Canada* outlines the results of a study of immigrants and their adjustment to Canada during their first three years in the country. The first volume, *Immigration Policy Perspectives* lays out the possible courses of action. The other volumes, all important in their own right, offer the background and material on which the first volume is based.

In addition to supplying the statistics and data on recent immigration and an overview of immigration administration and adjustment operations, the Green Paper also pinpoints important characteristics of recent immigration and Canadian population growth. Several factors are emphasized. Canada, the Green Paper explains, remains among those countries most open to immigration. Immigration restrictions and bars against accepting immigrants are being erected in countries like Australia, which had previously acted as a magnet for immigration. As a result, Canada falls under increasing pressure from would-be migrants seeking a new home who might earlier have considered going elsewhere. Immigrants who enter Canada tend to be unevenly distributed across the country. As many as 38 percent of all immigrants to Canada have come to the Toronto area during the year preceding the Green Paper's publication. More than 50 percent made their homes in southern Ontario. Immigrants overwhelmingly move into increasingly crowded urban centers. Very few go to the north or to farms. Most are absorbed into the English-language stream, even in Quebec, which views immigrant choice of English as a problem. In recent years the proportion of immigrants coming to Canada from traditional sources like Western Europe and the United States has fallen off. There has, however, been a sharp increase in immigration to Canada from the third world—South America, the Caribbean, and India/Pakistan.

Whether this last change will generate any racial friction in the future is unclear to the authors of the Green Paper. The Green Paper states, "In the circumstances it would be astonishing if there was no concern about the capacity of our society to adjust to a pace of population change that entails, after all, as regards international migration, novel and distinctive features." It goes on to point out, however, that Canada has a good record of adjusting to different immigrant groups and argues that any future immigration act reject the use of race and ethnicity as factors in determining immigration eligibility.

To elaborate on these and related characteristics of the current Canadian immigration scene, the Green Paper puts forward four basic options open to the government in determining future immigration policy and administration.

1. Retain the present immigration policy and immigration administration which neither limits numbers of immigrants entering Canada nor their place of origin. Existing legislation is designed to encourage family reunion on the one hand, allowing Canadians to bring relatives into Canada, while on the other, it seeks to find independent applicants who will become self-supporting and successful in establishing themselves in Canada on the basis of their skills, knowledge, or other qualifications. These independent applicants are assessed according to such criteria as age, education, health, the need for their particular skills in Canada, and their knowledge of English or French. Points are given in each area and if an applicant has enough points he is free to enter Canada as an immigrant.

2. Gear the immigration policy to meet the needs of Canada's economic and labor market policies. That is, only seek out or encourage the entry of those potential settlers who can fill immediate economic needs of Canada. In this way immigration would be tied to job vacancies or demand for workers in

specific fields. Immigrants would not be free to work where they want in Canada, but would be required to go to a specific job.

3. Establish definite quotas of immigrants from throughout the world. Canadian authorities would decide how many immigrants Canada could absorb each year and divide up this number on a worldwide or regional basis. The total number of immigrants allowed to enter each year would be fixed in advance and made up of no more than a specified number from different parts of the world.

4. Establish a quota based on priority needs of Canada. The quotas would not be set by geography but by Canadian demand for specific types of immigrants and the talents or skills they might offer. Preference would be shown to a predetermined number of applicants in fields Canada needs each year, whether the demand be for skilled craftsmen of one type one year and unskilled laborers in another field the next year. Those needed this year could well be excluded the next year.

With the exception of the first option, the ability of persons in Canada to bring relatives into Canada who do not meet the exact standards demanded would be sharply cut, especially for more distant relatives.

Public interest in the Green Paper was greater even than the government expected. Information Canada's first printing of 5,000 copies of the Green Paper costing $12.25 per set sold out almost immediately. A hurried second printing disappeared almost as quickly. Information Canada was hard pressed to keep up with a demand from eager readers.

In spite of this interest the four-volume Green Paper is not, according to the Minister, a statement of government policy. Quite the opposite. It is a discussion paper, an analysis of issues relating to Canadian immigration and population growth. Rather than make any one recommendation, it poses possible options for future immigration policy based upon the findings of this yearlong study. The options, the Minister hoped, would all be considered by the Canadian public in an organized public debate. The government, in turn, would await the results of this public debate before introducing new legislation or developing future policies.

The public debate called for by the Minister of Manpower and Immigration was not long in starting, although it did not always take the form he might have wanted. Reasoned discussion was to give way to passionate arguments, to protest demonstrations, shouting matches and, at times, the threat of violent confrontation between opposing sides.

In order to organize what it hoped would be an organized public debate on the Green Paper and the policy options it outlines, the government established a Special Parliamentary Committee on Immigration under the chairmanship of Martin O'Connell, Liberal Member of Parliament for the Toronto riding of Scarborough East.

The Committee traveled across Canada from city to city, holding public hearings into immigration. It invited organizations and individuals to come forward prepared to discuss the issues raised. Almost immediately, it was the Green Paper on Immigration Policy and the motives of the government in commissioning the document which became the subject of public debate.

Groups as varied as the Metropolitan Toronto Social Planning Council and the Canadian Communist Party questioned the government's wisdom in releasing the Green Paper to public debate. Some have charged that the Green Paper unnecessarily raises the issue of race and might even be racist in itself, promoting an antiblack and anti-oriental point of view. Some groups fear that the Green Paper is designed to divert attention away from Canada's economic problems into a phony debate on immigration, perhaps even to blame immigrants for

108

Canada's economic ills. Others charge that the government, or, more particularly, immigration officials, have already decided to introduce legislation which will effectively close immigration into Canada from the third world, thus cutting off most of the black and oriental immigration. This could be done, some claim, in many ways, including the use of those options which would tie immigration to skills (that would probably discriminate against less skilled persons from underdeveloped countries) or a quota system favoring the white countries.

Some of those who attack the Green Paper because they feel it makes immigrants and immigration an unnecessary target of debate would rather see a national debate on economic policy. Any discussion of immigration diverts national attention away from what they believe to be the real national problems—unemployment, unequal distribution of wealth, and foreign ownership of resources. To argue over immigration policy is, some contend, only making immigration appear to be a cause of Canada's economic ills. It would, in effect, prejudice the general public's attitude toward immigration when it is the current government's economic policies that are seen as the real villain.

Whenever the Special Parliamentary Committee on Immigration traveled they met two groups, those who wished to discuss the Green Paper and the options it presents and those who wished to protest the Green Paper as part of a government plan to both close off nonwhite immigration and cover up existing economic problems in a debate on immigration.

Hearings were often stormy and one held in Hamilton, Ontario, at the Sheraton-Connaught Hotel on 12 June 1975 proved no exception. An afternoon meeting which included comments from Hamilton's mayor had been peaceful enough—certainly more peaceful than those held a few days earlier in Toronto where angry exchanges took place between different groups attending the hearings, later spreading to include members of the Parliamentary Committee. The climax was reached when the Toronto Western Guard, a group dedicated to a white supremacy platform preaching hostility to nonwhites and Jews, attempted to present a brief against nonwhite immigrants. In the packed room, they could barely be heard above the catcalls of a hostile audience. One Committee member, Robert Kaplan, Liberal Member of Parliament for the Toronto riding of York Centre, walked out rather than listen to the racist Western Guard brief. Police were everywhere.

From Toronto the Committee moved on to Hamilton for afternoon and evening meetings. The 200 people who attended the evening meeting in Hamilton were again far from sympathetic to the government's Green Paper debate. Ann Brown, a member of the McMaster University Student Council, who delivered a statement attacking the debate as an effort to direct attention away from national economic issues, was given a standing ovation by the crowd. She was followed by Rolf Gurtzenberg who attacked the Green Paper as a racist document. According to a *Globe and Mail* report, he accused the government of wishing to "promote racist and fascist ideas." When a Committee member demanded Gurtzenberg apologize for the remark, the crowd stood up and began chanting and stamping their feet. As the chairman attempted to reestablish order and gain Mr. Gurtzenberg's apology, about fifty spectators began to chant "Withdraw the Green Paper, withdraw the Green Paper." Whatever hopes the Committee had of hearing any new speakers was now gone.

Mr. Gurtzenberg, who refused to retract his attack on the government, was ordered ejected from the hearings at the hands of hotel security men. A woman in the audience reached the microphone to protest but the microphone was turned off. She tried to turn it on again only to have the Committee Chairman grab it away. The meeting was nothing more than a shambles.

Committee members walked out and hotel staff turned out the lights, leaving the seventy-five or so people who remained throughout the disturbance sitting in the dark. They soon left and the meeting was over for the evening.

The Issues

• Who should be allowed to enter Canada as an immigrant?

The Green Paper on Immigration Policy
• Is there need for the government to reconsider immigration policy?

• Is the idea of a national debate on the Green Paper and immigration good? Why or why not?

• Would you expect the government to organize national debates on all issues which concern the public? Would it be a good idea to have organized public debates on the following?
  –capital punishment
  –abortion
  –tax rates
  –bilingualism
  –customs regulations
  –oil and gas prices
  –foreign ownership

• How or why do you think the issue of immigration is similar to or different from these other issues of public concern?

• Should a democratically elected government revise or pass laws, including new immigration legislation, on its own authority and without a formal public debate? Why or why not?

Population Size

• What do you think of Canada's current population size?

  –too small

  –too big

  –just about right

• What factors did you consider in deciding on your answer?

• Should Canada's population growth be controlled?

• What weight do you believe should be given to each of these issues in determining immigration policy? What importance should be given to each issue?

  –current birth rate

  –proportion of current population under 20 years of age

  –proportion of current population over 50 years of age

  –amount of arable land

  –unemployment rate and labor demand

  –housing costs

  –the pressure of hungry people in other parts of the world

• Does Canada have an obligation to accept any of the following people? Why or why not?

  –citizens of all Commonwealth countries

  –parents and grandparents of those already in Canada

  –brothers and sisters of those already in Canada

  –uncles, aunts, and cousins of those already in Canada

  –people fleeing persecution

  –people from areas with food shortages

  –people with university degrees

  –people seeking further education

• Canada admitted thousands of political refugees from Hungary after 1956, from Czechoslovakia after 1967, Uganda in 1972, and Chile in 1973. Should Canada open its doors to the following groups? Why or why not?

  –Palestinian refugees

112

—Jewish refugees from Arab countries
—Hong Kong refugees from the People's Republic of China
—Cuban refugees
—American draft resisters

• When Canada admits refugees from politically troubled areas or refugees from hunger, which individuals should get preference? Explain your choice.
—first come, first served
—the sick, the old, and the poor
—persons who are young and healthy
—the well educated or highly skilled
—those with relatives already in Canada
—those who have money to support themselves in Canada
—those who speak either English or French

• Who do you believe should decide what size Canada's population should be in the future?
—the voters
—politicians in parliament
—economists
—pollution experts

Distribution of Immigrants in Canada

• Should immigrants admitted into Canada be allowed to choose where they want to live? Explain your answer.

• Should prospective immigrants to Canada get preference if they go to areas of the country requiring additional population?

• Should prospective immigrants be excluded unless they will go to such areas?

• Is it fair to make immigrants go to areas where Canadian citizens will not go? Why or why not?

• Should Canadian-born people be required to live where the government feels population is needed?

113

• If going to a specific location is a condition of admission to Canada, what should be done to those immigrants who move away from that location?
   −nothing
   −send them back to their specified location
   −deport them
   −put them in jail
   −refuse to grant them citizenship
   −another solution. Specify.

• Should immigrants who become citizens be free to move to any place they want in Canada?

Employment
• Should immigration into Canada depend on an applicant having a desirable skill?

• Should immigrants be brought in to do jobs Canadians do not want to do? Why or why not?

• If Canada needs doctors and doctors apply to enter Canada, should they be admitted as immigrants:
   −if they don't speak English or French?
   −if they are over 65 years of age?
   −if they come from a country which has its own shortage of doctors?
   −if they will require a period of retraining to adjust to Canadian methods? Who should pay for retraining?

• Would your views about doctors as immigrants in these cases also apply to lawyers, plumbers, teachers, and carpenters who want to immigrate to Canada?

• What are the advantages and disadvantages of rejecting doctors from foreign countries instead of expanding Canadian medical schools to meet the needs of Canada?
   −Does rejecting doctors discriminate against doctors as immigrants?
   −Does it hurt Canadian taxpayers, who cover the cost of medical education in Canada, when we could get doctors free from other countries?

–Does it prevent Canadian children from eventually becoming doctors?

• Should immigrants to Canada have a job waiting before they are admitted? Why or why not? If so, what should be done with an immigrant who quits his job and takes a position that a Canadian citizen wanted? What should be done if an immigrant is fired? If he gets sick?

• Once an immigrant is in Canada should his employer, his union, or the government regard his employment conditions differently than for a Canadian citizen?

Race and Ethnicity
• Should race or nationality be a factor in the selection of immigrants for Canada?

• Should the present proportions of racial, religious, ethnic, and language groups be maintained by immigration? Explain your answer.

• How do you believe that Canadian society would be affected by each of the following immigration situations:
   –long-term immigration to Canada from the Caribbean which would raise the proportion of blacks in Canada from 150,000 to 300,000? to 500,000? to 1,000,000?
   –long-term immigration which would raise the number in the Italian ethnic community of Toronto from about 400,000 to 800,000?
   –long-term immigration which would raise the number of Jews in Canada from 300,000 to 600,000? to 1,600,000?
   –long-term immigration to Canada which would reduce the French-Canadian proportion of the population from about one-third of the total to one-quarter? to one-tenth?

• Do you think these growth situations are desirable, undesirable, or irrelevant? Why or why not?

• How do you think you would respond to each of these immigration changes under the following conditions? What issues would concern you? Which would not?
  – You are a French-speaking Canadian living in Quebec City.
  – You are an English-speaking Canadian living in Quebec City.
  – You live in Toronto. Moncton. Rural Manitoba.

• Should Canada have a quota system by race, religion, nationality, or ethnicity? If so, why? If not, why not?

• How do you think racial, religious, or ethnic groups in Canada would respond to such a quota?

• How do you believe other countries look at such a quota system? If the quota system was designed to maintain present population proportions, do you think Canada's international reputation would change?
  – in Jamaica
  – in the Philippines
  – in Norway
  – in Australia

• In setting its immigration policy should Canada consider the views of other countries? Why or why not?

• The federal government and Quebec are both dedicated to maintaining the French language, especially in Quebec. Should persons who speak French be given special advantages if they will settle in Quebec? If they will settle anywhere else in Canada?

• The birth rate among French-Canadians has fallen in recent years. Should immigration be used as much as possible to keep the French-language group in Canada (or Quebec) at the same proportion as it is today? Should it be used to increase the proportion of French-speaking people? Why or why not?

116

The Incident in Hamilton

• Immigration is obviously a very sensitive topic. Should the Special Parliamentary Committee on Immigration have been prepared for protest demonstrations?

• How should the Committee have been prepared for possible demonstrations?

• Do you think the protests are justified or unjustified? Why?

• Should groups such as the Western Guard be heard? Should they be allowed to make anti-black or anti-Jewish attacks?

• Should radical Marxist groups be heard? Should they be permitted to attack the existing economic system?

• Should individuals with no apparent affiliation be permitted to speak?

• Do you believe the right to freedom of speech protects people who make racist comments? Explain your answer.

• Should the statement by Mr. Gurtzenberg have been allowed? Should Mr. Gurtzenberg have apologized to the chairman?

• Was the chairman right to eject him?

• Was it correct for the Committee to walk out once the demonstration started? What else could they have done?

APPENDIX A

An Act for the Recognition and Protection of Human Rights and Fundamental Freedoms *

[*Assented to 10 August, 1960.*]

The Parliament of Canada, affirming that the Canadian Nation is founded upon principles that acknowledge the supremacy of God, the dignity and worth of the human person and the position of the family in a society of free men and free institutions;

Affirming also that men and institutions remain free only when freedom is founded upon respect for moral and spiritual values and the rule of law;

And being desirous of enshrining these principles and the human rights and fundamental freedoms derived from them, in a Bill of Rights which shall reflect the respect of Parliament for its constitutional authority and which shall ensure the protection of these rights and freedoms in Canada:

Therefore Her Majesty, by and with the advice and consent of the Senate and House of Commons of Canada, enacts as follows:

Statutes of Canada, 1960, Volume I, Chapter 44 (Ottawa: The Queen's Printer and Controller of Stationery, 1960). Reproduced by permission of Information Canada.

Part 1

Bill of Rights

1. It is hereby recognized and declared that in Canada there have existed and shall continue to exist without discrimination by reason of race, national origin, colour, religion or sex, the following human rights and fundamental freedoms, namely,

(*a*) the right of the individual to life, liberty, security of the person and enjoyment of property, and the right not to be deprived thereof except by due process of law;

(*b*) the right of the individual to equality before the law and the protection of the law;

(*c*) freedom of religion;

(*d*) freedom of speech;

(*e*) freedom of assembly and association; and

(*f*) freedom of the press.

2. Every law of Canada shall, unless it is expressly declared by an Act of the Parliament of Canada that it shall operate notwithstanding the *Canadian Bill of Rights*, be so construed and applied as not to abrogate, abridge or infringe or to authorize the abrogation, abridgement or infringement of any of the rights or freedoms herein recognized and declared, and in particular, no law of Canada shall be construed or applied so as to

(*a*) authorize or effect the arbitrary detention, imprisonment or exile of any person;

(*b*) impose or authorize the imposition of cruel and unusual treatment or punishment;

(*c*) deprive a person who has been arrested or detained

(i) of the right to be informed promptly of the reason for his arrest or detention,

(ii) of the right to retain and instruct counsel without delay, or

(iii) of the remedy by way of *habeas corpus* for the determination of the validity of his detention

and for his release if the detention is not lawful;
(*d*) authorize a court, tribunal, commission, board or other authority to compel a person to give evidence if he is denied counsel, protection against self crimination or other constitutional safeguards;
(*e*) deprive a person of the right to a fair hearing in accordance with the principles of fundamental justice for the determination of his rights and obligations;
(*f*) deprive a person charged with a criminal offence of the right to be presumed innocent until proved guilty according to law in a fair and public hearing by an independent and impartial tribunal, or of the right to reasonable bail without just cause; or
(*g*) deprive a person of the right to the assistance of an interpreter in any proceedings in which he is involved or in which he is a party or a witness, before a court, commission, board or other tribunal, if he does not understand or speak the language in which such proceedings are conducted.

3. The Minister of Justice shall, in accordance with such regulations as may be prescribed by the Governor in Council, examine every proposed regulation submitted in draft form to the Clerk of the Privy Council pursuant to the *Regulations Act* and every Bill introduced in or presented to the House of Commons, in order to ascertain whether any of the provisions thereof are inconsistent with the purposes and provisions of this Part and he shall report any such inconsistency to the House of Commons at the first convenient opportunity.

4. The provisions of this Part shall be known as the *Canadian Bill of Rights*.

Part II

5. (1) Nothing in Part I shall be construed to abrogate or abridge any human right or fundamental freedom not enumerated therein that may have existed in Canada at the commencement of this Act.

(2) The expression "law of Canada" in Part I means an Act of the Parliament of Canada enacted before or after the coming into force of this Act, any order, rule or regulation thereunder, and any law in force in Canada or in any part of Canada at the commencement of this Act that is subject to be repealed, abolished or altered by the Parliament of Canada.

(3) The provisions of Part I shall be construed as extending only to matters coming within the legislative authority of the Parliament of Canada.

6. Section 6 of the *War Measures Act* is repealed and the following substituted therefor:

"6. (1) Sections 3, 4 and 5 shall come into force only upon the issue of a proclamation of the Governor in Council declaring that war, invasion or insurrection, real or apprehended, exists.

(2) A proclamation declaring that war, invasion or insurrection, real or apprehended, exists shall be laid before Parliament forthwith after its issue, or, if Parliament is then not sitting, within the first fifteen days next thereafter that Parliament is sitting.

(3) Where a proclamation has been laid before Parliament pursuant to subsection (2), a notice of motion in either House signed by ten members thereof and made in accordance with the rules of that House within ten days of the day the proclamation was laid before Parliament, praying that the proclamation be revoked, shall be debated in that House at the first convenient opportunity within the four sitting days next after the day the motion in that House was made.

(4) If both Houses of Parliament resolve that the proclamation be revoked, it shall cease to have effect, and sections 3, 4 and 5 shall cease to be in force until those sections are again brought into force by a further proclamation but without prejudice to the previous operation of those sections or anything duly done or suffered thereunder or any offence committed or any

penalty or forfeiture or punishment incurred.

(5) Any act or thing done or authorized or any order or regulation made under the authority of this Act, shall be deemed not to be an abrogation, abridgement or infringement of any right or freedom recognized by the *Canadian Bill of Rights.*"

BIBLIOGRAPHY

Allport, Gordon. *The Nature of Prejudice.* Cambridge, Mass.: Addison-Wesley Press, 1950.

Bennett, John W. *Hutterian Brethren.* Stanford: Stanford University Press, 1967.

Boissevain, Jeremy. *The Italians of Montreal.* Ottawa: Queen's Printer, 1970.

Canada. Department of Manpower and Immigration. *Immigration and Population Statistics.* Ottawa: Information Canada, 1975.

Canada. Department of Manpower and Immigration. *Immigration Policy Perspectives.* Ottawa: Information Canada, 1975.

Canada. Department of Manpower and Immigration. *The Immigration Program.* Ottawa: Information Canada, 1975.

Canada. Department of Manpower and Immigration. *Three Years in Canada.* Ottawa: Information Canada, 1975.

Canada. Royal Commission on Bilingualism and Biculturalism. *The Cultural Contribution of the Other Ethnic Groups.* Ottawa: Queen's Printer, 1970.

Clairmont, Donald H., and Magill, Dennis W. *Africville: The Life and Death of a Canadian Black Community.* Toronto: McClelland and Stewart, 1974.

Cook, Ramsay, ed. *French Canadian Nationalism: An Anthology.* Toronto: Macmillan, 1969.

Corbett, David C. *Canada's Immigration Policy: A Critique*. Toronto: University of Toronto Press, 1957.

Davis, M., and Krauter, J. F. *The Other Canadians: Profiles of Six Minorities*. Toronto: Methuen, 1971.

Eisenberg John, and Troper, Harold. *Native Survival*. Toronto: Ontario Institute for Studies in Education, 1973.

Elliot, Jean, ed. *Minority Canadians: Immigrant Groups*. Toronto: Prentice-Hall, 1971.

Gordon, Milton. *Assimilation in American Life*. New York: Oxford University Press, 1964.

Harney, Robert, and Troper, Harold. *Immigrants: A Portrait of the Urban Experience, 1890-1930*. Toronto: Van Nostrand Reinhold, 1975.

Hawkins, Freda. *Canada and Immigration: Public Policy and Public Concern*. Montreal: McGill–Queen's University Press, 1972.

Hostetler, John A., and Huntington, Gertrude. *The Hutterites of North America*. New York: Holt, Rinehart and Winston, 1967.

Hughes, David R., and Koller, Evelyn. *The Anatomy of Racism: Canadian Dimensions*. Montreal: Harvest House, 1974.

Kalbach, Warren E. *The Impact of Immigration on Canada's Population*. Ottawa: Dominion Bureau of Statistics, 1970.

Lieberson, Stanley. *Language and Ethnic Relations in Canada*. New York: John Wiley, 1970.

McDiarmid, Garnet, and Pratt, David. *Teaching Prejudice*. Toronto: Ontario Institute for Studies in Education, 1971.

Morten, James. *In the Sea of Sterile Mountains*. Vancouver: J. J. Douglas, 1974.

Norris, John, ed. *Strangers Entertained: A History of the Ethnic Groups of British Columbia*. Vancouver: British Columbia Centennial '71 Committee, 1971.

Palmer, Howard. *Immigration and the Rise of Multiculturalism*. Toronto: Copp Clark, 1975.

———. *Land of the Second Chance: A History of Ethnic Groups in Southern Alberta*. Lethbridge: Lethbridge Herald, 1972.

Porter, John A. *The Vertical Mosaic: An Analysis of Social Class and Power in Canada*. Toronto: University of Toronto Press, 1965.

Troper, Harold M. *Only Farmers Need Apply: Official Canadian Government Encouragement of Immigration from the United States.* Toronto: Griffin House, 1972.

Winks, Robin W. *The Blacks in Canada: A History.* Montreal: McGill–Queen's University Press, 1971.

Yuzyk, Paul. *Ukrainian Canadians: Their Place and Role in Canadian Life.* Toronto: Ukrainian Canadian Business and Professional Federation, 1967.

Films

Bilingualism. B&W. 29 mins. NFB. An examination of the question of bilingualism as it affects a large corporation in Quebec.

Born Black. B&W. 50 mins. International Telefilm. Presents the history of black immigration and settlement in Canada and reflects on the problems and discrimination that blacks face when seeking employment and housing.

Canada: Unity or Division. Color. 23 mins. NBC. A case study of the problems of a French-Canadian minority in an English-speaking land.

A Day in the Night of Jonathan Mole. B&W. 29 mins. NFB. A frank discussion of the causes and consequences of racial prejudice particularly as it restricts a man's chances for employment.

Encounter at Kwaiha House—Halifax. B&W. 18 mins. NFB. A group of black and white youths gather racial, discrimination, and educational issues in Halifax.

Everybody's Prejudiced. B&W. 21 mins. NFB. A film which explores the nature of prejudice through examples which everyone can recognize and discuss.

The Hutterites. B&W. 28 mins. NFB. A film made on a Hutterite colony in Alberta showing all aspects of Hutterite daily life.

The Italian in Transition. Color. 26 mins. International Telefilm. A film exploring the problems and experiences of Italian immigrants on coming to Canada, with special reference to their schooling in Italy and Canada.

Manitoba: Festival Country. Color. 27 mins. Manitoba Government Film Library. The film looks into the ethnic groups and cultural backgrounds of the people who now make up Manitoba.

Our Street Was Paved with Gold. Color. 28 mins. NFB. An often nostalgic film looking into an urban immigrant neighborhood and the changes it has undergone over the years.

This Business of Immigration. Color. 60 mins. OECA. A survey of Canadian immigration and attitudes toward immigrants, using humor, animation, and historical material.

The Threshold. B&W. 23 mins. NFB. A portrayal of the adjustments—easy and difficult—faced by every immigrant family upon its first contact with the schools.

To Find a House. B&W. 29 mins. Anti-Defamation League of the B'nai B'rith. Details the experiences of a black American family's unsuccessful efforts to find an apartment in a middle-sized city.

CBC Audio Tapes

Bilingualism: Rags and Riches. Cat. no. 249. 1 hour. A documentary that explores problems of bilingualism including the dilemmas faced by non-English-speaking immigrants who come to Canada.

The Bill of Rights: Help or Hindrance. Cat. no. 437L. 1 hour. Questions the place of the Bill of Rights in defending the rights of individuals and minority groups and attempts to analyze the place of courts in defending these rights.

The Blacks in Canada. Cat. no. 665. 30 mins. An interview with Burnley "Rocky" Jones, a controversial Halifax black community leader, and his thoughts on blacks in Canada.

Canada: Melting Pot or Mosaic? Cat. no. 656. 30 mins. A program contrasting the traditional U.S. and Canadian models for immigrant absorption—the Melting Pot and the Mosaic.

Immigrants to Power. Cat. no. 797. 1 hour. Explores the ability of immigrants to move into the Canadian power structure and become part of the existing hierarchy.

OTHER TITLES IN THIS SERIES

Available from General Publishing Co. Ltd., 30 Lesmill Road, Don Mills, Ontario M3B 2T6:

Don't Teach That! An exploration of areas such as religious education in which teaching in schools touches upon questions of strong personal conviction.

Foreign Ownership. The problems and issues arising from the extensive foreign ownership of business corporations in Canada.

The Law and the Police. Recent cases illustrating the controversy that results when the rights of the individual clash with the process of law enforcement.

Rights of Youth. Situations where conflict arises between the responsibilities of schools and the rights of young people.

Available from Publications Sales, OISE, 252 Bloor Street West, Toronto, Ontario M5S 1V6:

Native Survival. The dilemma of Canada's Indians as the culture and laws of the majority threaten their way of life and their group identity.

Crisis in Quebec. The rise of the Front de Libération du Québec and the events of October 1970 are examined in the political context of Quebec.

On Strike! Several labor-management confrontations of recent years in Canada examined in the light of their impact on workers, business, and the public.

The Right to Live and Die. Case studies around such issues as abortion, sterilization, euthanasia, and capital punishment as they concern the individual, the society, and the law.

Women in Canadian Society. Recent cases on women and work, women and the law, and native women consider claims for equal status with men in these areas.